Psychoanalysis, Neu the Stories of Our L

Psychoanalysis, Neuroscience and the Stories of Our Lives: The Relational Roots of Mental Health offers a new understanding of identity and mental health, shining the light of twenty-first century neurobiology on the core tenets of psychoanalysis. Accessibly written, it outlines the great leaps forward in neuroscience over the past three decades, and the consequent implications for understanding mental health symptoms today.

Central to the book is the idea that the seeds of mental illness are discovered not in the individual's own fallibilities, but in the complex relationships we experience from our very first moments. Integrating the latest neuroscientific research, it depicts the individual as inherently interdependent with their environment, their neurobiological and emotional foundations framed by the context in which they are raised. Integrating traditional psychoanalytic ideas with findings from neurobiology and neuroscience, it reframes the Oedipal setup, examines clinical depression as the presence of absence, and revisits resistance and the neurobiology of denial. Weaving narratives drawn from clinical practice, and highlighting implications for contemporary lives, the book is a tour de force, smashing the myth that our minds develop separately from the world around us.

This clear, lucid book, providing a timely overview of emotional and neurobiological development, will appeal to both psychologists and psychoanalysts. It will be also be a key reference work for mental health professionals, particularly those working in early years services.

Dr Sarah Sutton has thirty years' experience of working with parents, children and adolescents who have suffered adversity and are struggling behaviourally and emotionally. She is author of *Being Taken In: The Framing Relationship* (Karnac, 2014), and has co-edited the *Journal of Child Psychotherapy*. She is also the founder of Understanding Children and co-founder of the Learning Studio, teaching, writing and working on the interface between development research and psychoanalytic ideas.

"This book provides an innovative and impressive synthesis of neurobiological and developmental research with in-depth psychoanalytic thinking, a synthesis which has profound implications, both for clinical work but also for our understanding of life in general, a text for which clinicians and those generally interested in the challenges of being human, will be extremely grateful."

– Graham Music PhD, Consultant Child and Adolescent Psychotherapist at the Tavistock and Portman Clinics, adult psychotherapist in private practice and author of *Nurturing Children* (2019), *The Good Life* (2014) and *Nurturing Natures* (2011)

"Sarah Sutton is a terrific writer. Her writing is full of seemingly casual but hugely powerful zest. She happens also to be a gifted artist and she somehow makes the links between these two, usually exceedingly difficult, subjects of psychoanalysis and science totally accessible, alive, exciting and beautiful."

– Anne Alvarez PhD, MACP, Consultant Child and Adolescent Psychotherapist

"This accessible integration of psychoanalytic theory and interpersonal neurobiology puts relationships at the heart of development and the creation of personal meaning. Together these two approaches are used to open a creative perspective on the formation and workings of the mind and how, when needed, help may be offered. Babies employ the skills needed to relate from birth, although they do not know it, and relationships with parents sway the consolidation of important neural networks during infancy (and also, but less so, beyond) that are the foundations upon which the development of the psyche must build. When significant relationships are inimical to healthy development, or missing, small children cannot escape by themselves and so must endure and adapt. They know no alternative, and without intervention may eventually base their sense of self on this survival software. This is a matter of unconscious hardwired expectations of the moment to come that bias how the world is comprehended and generate a reaction before now is even noticed. A symptom has been distilled from a role that had to be played within a family drama. As this book shows, only with in-depth understanding allied with compassionate and considered relationships can such misplaced responses to a past environment of difficult relationships be changed."

– Robin Balbernie, Infant Mental Health Specialist; Child and Adolescent Psychotherapist

"This is the book we have been waiting for, a riveting work by Sarah Sutton, who is witty in writing about serious issues, law-abiding and revolutionary. She writes with respect about psychoanalysis and makes connections with ground-breaking neuroscience and relational psychotherapy, helping to fill the gaps between them. She illuminates the book with both poetry and science. She talks of 'silent understanding' and reading the book gives an experience of this. It is both comforting and inspiring. It confronts the modern dilemma that mental health difficulties lead to more referrals than can ever be met by clinicians, and optimistically shows that thinking relationally, not just individually, can take the pathology out of mental health, and generate a fuller understanding which helps regulation and recovery. The book helps us understand better not only ourselves, but also the communities we live in."

–Dilys Daws, Honorary Consultant Child Psychotherapist at the Tavistock and Portman Clinics, Founding Chair of the Association for Infant Mental Health UK and co-author of *Finding Your Way With Your Baby* (2015), First Prize in Popular Medicine, BMA Medical Books Awards 2016

Psychoanalysis, Neuroscience and the Stories of Our Lives

The Relational Roots of Mental Health

Sarah Sutton

Routledge
Taylor & Francis Group
LONDON AND NEW YORK

First published 2020
by Routledge
2 Park Square, Milton Park, Abingdon, Oxon OX14 4RN

and by Routledge
52 Vanderbilt Avenue, New York, NY 10017

Routledge is an imprint of the Taylor & Francis Group, an informa business

British Library Cataloguing-in-Publication Data
A catalogue record for this book is available from the British Library

Library of Congress Cataloging-in-Publication Data
A catalog record has been requested for this book

ISBN: 978-1-138-36429-5 (hbk)
ISBN: 978-1-138-36430-1 (pbk)
ISBN: 978-0-429-43145-6 (ebk)

Typeset in Times New Roman
by Integra Software Services Pvt. Ltd.

For my parents, who taught me all they knew
and my children, who have shown me a new world

Contents

Foreword

This book has taken six months and six years to write. Those years were mostly spent looking, thinking, reading, and plucking up my courage. Although I found in psychoanalysis a conversation I had been looking for all my life, it sometimes seemed as if I was eavesdropping on a conversation that I should not dare to join – .or only on terms of engagement that were set long ago. The idea of Freud is beyond human; he is monumental, and perhaps all we can do is worship at the shrine and write footnotes to his vast oeuvre. But the more I read of the development research, the more there was something I wanted to say. It may be a footnote, but perhaps it may serve too as a stumbling block: in the psychoanalytic tradition, it seems to me, something about what it is to be a child has been sacrificed.

It has become clear that some profound psychoanalytic insights are neurobiologically valid. There is though, an important shift of emphasis towards the mutual construction of meaning. Emotionality is physiologically reciprocal, and associated meanings – and the capacity to make meaning – are wired in relationally through neural connections in our first thousand days. In the world of child psychotherapy, we cannot now accuse our child selves of hating links, for example, and hating meaning, without understanding that this symptom arises through relational experience. Some of the diagnoses we have relied upon for many years make a different kind of sense in the context of the relational development of mind. What are we doing when we insist on seeing individuals, even individual children, even traumatized individual children, as responsible for their own mental health condition? We are projecting a social problem into society's most powerless members.

We can no longer avoid the knowledge that 'character' does not exist as an inbuilt disposition; rather our genes offer potentiality, switched on or off by experience of the world and the formative relationships in which our minds are made up. In the post-postmodern world, with our institutions, monuments, and frames of reference no longer taken for granted, the power of the setup more visible and open to question, we cannot turn a blind eye to the fact that frameworks for understanding, for feeling, for thinking, for living, are built through experience.

In thinking about some of the ideas in this book, the step outside the frame that psychoanalysis both necessitates and denies has been uncomfortable, putting me at one remove from the people around me. I would like to thank them and ask, in the words of Lee Israel, can you ever forgive me?

Acknowledgements

Without the following people, this book would have been much the worse, and might never have been written:

Anne Alvarez, who is a leading light and the reason I wanted to train to be a child psychotherapist; Robin Balbernie, who encouraged me from the beginning of my training to think outside the frame; Moira Keyes, whose insight and kindness have sustained me more than she knows; Maureen Begadon, for our searching conversations about everything over the years; Dilys Daws, whom I had the pleasure of getting to know and re-read as I wrote this; Judith Edwards, whose warm writerly encouragement I very much value; Luca D'Avanzo, whose perceptive and original perspective is always refreshing; Paul Barrows, Tessa Weir-Jeffrey, Gail Walker, and Jane Randall, my colleagues in Bristol who keep the show on the road with grace, humour & the occasional staff outing, my engaging students for our lively conversations, and of course Russell George, Elliott Morsia, and everyone at Routledge who gave this book the go ahead and helped it along the way.

Closer to home, the book and I have been shaped by my inimitable parents, Margaret and Mike, who play starring roles in the ongoing tragicomedy of our family life; Andrew, my husband, who stands beside me; my stepchildren Gwen, Sam and Harry, from whom I have learnt a great deal; my stoic sisters- and brothers-in-law, Trudi, Ros, SJ, and David, who put up with us all and without whom my lovely nieces and nephews would not be here; my brothers and sisters: Mick, our golden boy, who enjoyed his life, and faced his death with quiet courage; Paul, who has always been brainier than me though I have never admitted it; Beth, who can make anything and devotes herself to designing and sustaining a world for children to flourish in, and J, forever poised in my imagination intrepid on the high board. Finally, and above all, I want to thank my extraordinary grown up children and their partners: Joe, Nicole, Ellie, Mike, and Gabriel, who make the world a better place by being in it.

Introduction

A million neural connections a second are made in our first thousand days. T. S. Eliot's *Four Quartets* tell us how lifetimes burn in our every moment; the past three decades of brain research have made this insight incontestable. We are the place where poetry and science converge, our identities grounded in the connections made, the silent understandings gathered through patterns of relating in our families. This daily patterning weaves our understanding of what we are for; a sense of purpose, belonging, and identity protecting us from an isolation we would not survive. We experience ourselves as separate individuals, but are in fact in profound and continual call and response with the social and emotional world around us, and this responsive connection is shaped by our earliest relationships and their intergenerational influences. Undeciphered lifetimes burn in our every moment. The myth of the individual mind is now discredited by infant brain research, though widely promulgated for reasons we will consider later on. Our minds are shaped through connections with the people closest to us. When things go wrong, our mental health troubles are best understood in that context. However mystifying our symptoms may seem, put the missing people into the story of our lives, and what is played out in the theatre of our bodies begins to make sense.

I was born in northern England, but my DNA is the product of many journeys going back generations, from the west of Ireland, western Europe, and the Middle East; life stories that happened to connect in that particular place. We are each of us the opposite of a diaspora, a concentration of lives. The intergenerational load we carry is transmitted through every possible level of being, from the markers in our cells to the ways of being in our families and wider groups. It is time to start taking this human psychobiological truth into account in the way we see ourselves. We urgently need a response to increasingly widespread mental health problems that includes the missing people, and looks at the story the symptom is telling us.

Current psychological treatments largely ignore the unconscious. Many people are wary of Freud's ideas, and of course like the rest of us, he was a product of his own social and historical context. We are at risk of throwing the baby out with the bathwater though if we do not take unconscious undercurrents into account in our understanding of mental health, indeed of human behaviour. This is arguably Freud's greatest achievement, not to have discovered the unconscious, for ideas about it have run through philosophy and literature for centuries, but to have discovered it for science, and to have shown how unconscious conflicts that do not make the edit in the story of our lives come to light as symptoms. Many schools of psychoanalytic thought branch from the early days of the Wednesday evening group in Vienna at the turn of the last century, but I will chiefly draw in this book on the line of psychoanalytic thinking that leads from Freud, through Klein and Bion to Alvarez, who has incorporated development research into psychoanalytic theory and practice.

This more integrated contemporary psychoanalytic model is in accord with the neurologist Damasio's call for a new understanding of major causes of human suffering. Looking beyond cognition to emotionality, he asserts the therapeutic value of understanding the links between feeling, brain, and mind as 'indispensable to the future construction of a view of human beings more accurate than the one currently available' (Damasio, 2003:7). Neuroscience now confirms the presence of undercurrents of (un)awareness, coursing through the body, part of our own particular navigation system for being in the world.

We feel at home with these states of mind/body, even when they are painful, because home is where we start from, as Winnicott (1986) made clear. These are the states of mind holding sway in our earliest experience of home, back when our brains were hitting the ground running, making a million neural connections a second. We adapt to the way things are for us then in order to belong and survive: no baby survives in isolation. We learn through swimming in the prevailing currents, and take the way it feels for granted, like the fish in the African proverb who are the last to acknowledge the existence of water. Babies have no comparator, and no one explains to them the way things are. They take in the qualities of ways of being in the world around them without question, as part of where they belong.

It is the feeling of what happens, as Damasio (1999) puts it, that literally forms our state of mind through neurological connections. New neural pathways are formed in response to emotional and interpersonal stimuli. This gives us the basis for our experience of the world and our place in it; it is the ground we stand on. To suggest that any one of us is the source of our own mental health, has symptoms that can be understood out of context or can get better on our own through conscious effort is therefore not only misleading but cruel. Our ways of being, even as adults, are to be understood in the context of our family, indeed, of our family history, and the chances and pressures of its wider social context.

The internationally recognized Story Stem Assessment Profile, developed by the Anna Freud Centre, draws on this knowledge to inform court decisions about children's welfare. Children are offered the beginning of a story, and invited to continue it in any way they choose. What they show and tell offers a glimpse into the world they live in, in their heads but also in their outside world – the two are profoundly and interactively connected from birth. They are acting out in miniature aspects of their experience of relationships.

Odd as it may sound, as adults we do something rather similar. In conversation, we are offering other people a part in the play of our lives that has already been written. In what follows, I will offer evidence that shows how we discard responses that do not fit the script. However tiny, the bits that do fit will be seized upon as evidence validating our expectations. It turns out that the brain is not so much rational as rationalizing, making up a story we recognize as it goes along. I will draw on the science of perception to illustrate how this happens, how our perceptual system is in fact an 'anticipation machine' (Siegel, 1999), a mechanism of adaptation to our early environment. Once set, it functions as a navigation system, alerting us to dangers. If our early experience has not been too extreme, it will have wired in a navigation system that will fit most everyday encounters, and we will be seen as mentally healthy, able to relate to people in a way they can understand. We are seen as mentally ill when the wired-in template we are using only fits a very specific environment, so that we behave as if we are in a world that no one (outside our birth family) can understand. This behaviour can look like madness in any other context, but will have made sense and indeed offered important protection in that early world.

To all intents and purposes then, for good or ill, we inhabit the world of our early childhood. What I want to do in this book is show

how we can only really understand our own behaviour, especially when it is puzzling, in the context of that world and its relationships. Mental health symptoms tell their own tale. Put the missing people into the story, and it begins to make sense. For example, the sad little boy who could never be sure whether or not his mother would be available distracts himself as an adult man with betting huge sums on a particular outcome. The more enormous the sums involved, the more exciting the gamble. He can ride high on the risk instead of feeling powerless in the face of its horrible uncertainty. Obsessive Compulsive Disorder (OCD) could readily be labelled Locking the Door After the Horse has Bolted Syndrome. There has been an actual lapse in security, danger has got in, and the person with the OCD symptom was unable to prevent it. The security guard was missing, and the person is suffering now from that lack, which searches for expression. Feeling perhaps unconsciously or otherwise that they should have been able to be the security guard themselves, they embody that lack, impersonating the missing person, as it were. They continue to try to prevent damage that has already happened, doomed to repeat the failure until someone else realizes the danger they (or their parents) were in, still present to their mind. This interpretation fits with the characterization of the problem of OCD as the detection of error signals, giving rise to 'a persistent internal sense of something wrong' (Schwartz, 1999:113), provoking repeated attempts to rectify it. It is true – there was something wrong, it is just not about now. Or rather, it is about now, in the sense that the past inhabits the present, in a familiar setup, encountered again and again. What do we do about missing someone we cannot bear to miss? We tend to make them present, to re-present them in ways I will explore in the chapters that follow, either by embodying them or by subtly evoking them in others.

I intend then in this book to revisit some dearly held assumptions about mental health, indeed about the way human beings work and about how change happens. They are indeed dearly held; I will try to show how they are in fact expensive mistakes. In the light of the scientific knowledge discovered in the last three decades of brain research, I examine the surprisingly prevalent notion that individual conscious effort in itself can help people change for the better. In fact we are wired by and for relating, and it makes no sense to think of people as separate units, each in the driving seat of our own little self vehicle. The neuroscientist Eagleman compares consciousness to 'a tiny stowaway on a transatlantic steamship, taking credit for the journey without acknowledging the massive engineering underfoot' (2011:4). He explains:

> Your brain is built of cells called neurons and glia – hundreds of billions. Each one of these cells is as complicated as a city. And each one contains the entire human genome and traffics billions of molecules in intricate economies. Each cell sends electrical pulses to other cells, up to hundreds of times per second.
>
> (Eagleman, 2011:1)

Given this scale of activity, how could we possibly keep track of it all? Eagleman's suggestion is that the point of consciousness is to be like the Chief Executive Officer of a large organization, making decisions. These decisions draw on all kinds of perceptual information-streams, most of them unconscious, and pretty much dependent on previous experience as we will see – you could say we pursue the path we recognize.

In examining long held clinical assumptions about the human self and moving towards a new neurobiologically informed concept of the relational construction of identity and of mental health, we find ourselves in an intermediate area between a number of disciplines, including psychoanalysis, physiology, neurobiology, philosophy, social science, and developmental research. This betweenness of perspectives is itself a fractal example of the relational process in which meaning is constructed. We make connections; that is how our brain works. We are interested in relationships between, and we ignore these at our peril. Head down any one particular path and you lose sight of other possibilities. McGilchrist's (2009) important work on the relation between the left and right hemispheres of the brain shows how, essentially, the left brain is the hemisphere of what, seeing the snapshot, the specified content; the right brain is the hemisphere of how, apprehending the wave, the process, the flow of experience. He shows how and why we tend to privilege one over the other, citing twenty-first century western civilization as a warning. Focusing our attention on the what, rather than the how of experience distorts our development. The left brain is the site of grasp, in both the physical and the intellectual sense. It is the natural home of the agenda, which inevitably excludes what is unknown or uncertain. The left brain cannot capture what we might call the musicality of life, which is, after all, what makes life worth living. It disregards the joy of a harmonious connection or the frustrations and effort of a jangling disharmony. In mistaking the travel snap for the journey, the left brain misses the feeling of what happens, the music of qualities like pace, timing, rhythm, and intensity, which tend to belong to the right hemisphere. It misses the to and fro of betweenness, which creates the new, bringing the surprise of the unexpected.

This work and the huge range of research on the brain and the development of mind and self (Schore, 1994; Solms & Turnbull, 2002) over the past three decades facilitates the beginning of the new, more accurate view of human beings that Damasio (2003) has called for. It brings into question widely held assumptions about mental development and mental health, and brings the relational context into the foreground. It is no longer scientifically tenable to ignore this research and cling to the idea of personality as a given. It has become clear that any attempt to understand and address mental health problems is doomed to failure unless it includes the social, relational context and uses it as the mechanism of change.

Our justice system, for example, is set up to see individuals as responsible for crimes, and yet it is not a coincidence that crime is highest in areas of most deprivation; see the Index of Multiple Deprivation (2010) figures on the UK government website for the correlation. Jails are full of people who have been deprived early in the most formative years of their lives. This is not to say that everyone who is deprived ends up in jail; but it is to say that without help, those who have more vulnerability factors – being male is one, being undernourished, or frightened are others – are likely to suffer most long-term damaging consequences. In the UK, children growing up in the thirty most deprived local authorities have significantly worse health and development outcomes than those in the thirty least deprived areas. The knock-on effects of deprivation continue into adolescence and beyond:

> The presence of poverty in the lives of children and young people has been identified as a negative predictive factor that hinders their development – associated with such consequences as adolescent criminality, school dropout, teen pregnancy, and infant mortality.
>
> (Ferguson, 2008:8)

It is striking that we tend to delete awareness of contributing factors, and would rather put the responsibility on our children or our child selves for badness than on any factor in our relationship with a parent figure. We see this in the sentimentalizing of motherhood, for example. Considering infantile dependency, it makes sense to idealize the people we depend on, especially if they are unpredictable, even unreliable. It is very risky to bite the hand that feeds you, especially if you cannot be too sure of the feed. In this book, I will explore the neuroscience of the making of minds which sheds a different light on ideas about good and evil and where we locate them.

In the chapters that follow, I will try to show how stories about identity wired in through patterns of relating are diagnosed as disorders. I have drawn on clinically familiar experiences condensed into fictional identities to show how disordered patterns of relating, disordered histories, become stories about identity. We will see how, for good or ill, in our early days we wire in a navigation system adapted to the social group we are born into, which guides us, particularly when we are under stress, for the rest of our lives. It forms the basis not only of what we notice, what we value, but of who we feel ourselves to be.

Throughout the book, I examine the idea of mental health symptoms as having to do with failures of connection, with roots in incommunicable pain arising from traumatic experience. Trauma by definition is an embodied memory, an experienced truth that is unrepresented, unrepresentable in fact, in the context of the patient's life, other than by the symptom. I will try to show how madness can be understood as a symptom in search of meaning, which has yet to be taken in by another mind. The traumatic pain is lodged in the body at a pre-verbal level, and cannot be approached or expressed through words, but only through behaviour – the theatre of the body, as it were. A recent case that made the national papers in the UK, for example, concerned a boy who stabbed his teacher, saying, 'It was her or me'. His feeling seems to have been that 'her' survival was not compatible with his, and with the benefit of neuroscience, we can take the 'her' to stand for the earliest prototype female figure in his mind. In thinking later about the relational construction of identity, I will look at some of the roots of this feeling in postnatal experience, which for some mothers can feel just as extreme and polarized: it's the baby or me. If we take the relational growth of mind seriously, (and the research we look at here makes it hard to deny), the question of taking responsibility begins to look rather complex, and moral judgements become harder to make.

The relational roots of behaviour call into question the very nature of personal responsibility, which is worth a bit of examination here I think. The boy in question was assessed as being of sound mind, that is, could be held responsible. What does it mean in this context to say he was of sound mind? This judgement strikes me as odd and ill-informed; it ignores the neuroscience of how minds are wired, and evokes medieval notions of good and evil. Are we seriously suggesting he is intrinsically evil? You may as well say he was possessed by the devil. I guess the implicit meaning of attributing a sound mind to this boy is that he deserves punishment, which is not the same thing. We tend to problematize the person, even children, displaying symptoms, rather than the experience which has given rise to those symptoms. Witness the public relations campaign undertaken by the mother of Dylan Klebold, who killed thirteen people and himself at Columbine school. She seems in this campaign to have been desperately trying to protect an idea of her own goodness. Her son then becomes, tragically, the fall guy. Essentially, her stance seems to be that the badness is in him: 'It was him or me'. There's no getting away from it, despite our communal efforts to lay blame at any one individual door, the way people behave is essentially to be understood in a fundamentally relational context, which includes intergenerational family history. In the chapters that follow, I will try to show how a symptom can be understood as essentially a survival mechanism taken out of its own particular relational context. I will look at the implications for our sense of identity and its relationship with social context.

As Freud suggests, the boundaries of the self can be rather hard to distinguish:

> Pathology has made us acquainted with a great number of states in which the boundary lines between the ego and the external world become uncertain or in which they are actually drawn incorrectly. There are cases in which parts of a person's own body, even portions of his own mental life – his perceptions, thoughts and feelings – appear alien to him and as not belonging to his ego; there are other cases in which he ascribes to the external world things that clearly originate in his own ego and that ought to be acknowledged by it.
>
> (Freud, 1930:66)

The assertion here is that this blurring of the lines between persons is pathological; recent neurobiology has in fact found this phenomenon universally. Look at the function of mirror neurons (Rizzolatti & Craighero, 2004), which fire upon witnessing an action every bit as much as if we ourselves had performed it. What is me and what is not me is intersubjectively established in a kind of see-saw mutuality. As neighbouring states (of mind), our boundaries are much more provisional than they seem, and are continually subject to revision. As testament to this provisionality, consider the heavy compensation police had to pay when an undercover policeman had assumed an identity, and someone took him at face value to the extent of bearing his child. Given that he was present at the intensely real event of the birth, I can only assume that he believed in it, too, if only partially; at the very least, when he was in character, as it were. A very real son was born from this 'fictitious' relationship. It seems apparent, from this and from other evidence I will explore, that identity is a much more constructed, much more mutual process than we like to believe.

This raises the interesting question: who are we when we are being ourselves? Whose self is it anyway? It invites reconsideration of a number of key areas, familiar to psychoanalytic thinkers. If a template for the vast majority of our responses and expectations of relationships is laid down in early life, and is not available to consciousness for efficiency of processing, in psychoanalytic terms Bollas' 'unthought known' (1987), the stage is set for what is played out in the rest of our lives. The very work we do is often a metaphor for the work of our early relationships: as I have mentioned, the child of an unreliable parent may become a gambler, investing with a risk of no return; the child of a damaged mother becomes perhaps a gynaecologist, playing out a continuing need to heal her in the succession of women he treats who make present again in his life the original damaged 'her' in his mind.

In talking about identity, we need a way of talking about the edit, the account we give of ourselves. This way of talking needs to be situated between the worlds of art and of science, to acknowledge the interplay between the physiological and the imaginative. I will look at the symptom as the body's metaphor; an experienced truth-seeking expression, that has been deleted from the received version of the story. In searching for a new way of talking about human experience that does justice not only to the body/mind interrelation but also to the formative nature of social interrelation, I will explore the idea that the language of the body tells us what we do not know we know, as Eisold (2010) puts it.

In the opening chapter, 'What you see is what you get', we will look at how the neuroscience of perception helps us understand the relationship between seeing, being, and identity. McGilchrist (2009) alerts us to the shaping quality of attention, how what we see is what we think we 'get', take in, understand. The corollary is, we do not 'get' what we do not see, so that potential new pathways can be invisible to us as the familiar beckons time and again. I will draw on evidence from neurobiology to show how this system works, reinforcing neuronal connections that are used, and pruning those that are not. This has widespread and important implications for personal and social change.

Leading on from the distinction between awareness and unconscious perception, we will explore in the following chapter the function of behaviour as communication, particularly the potential gap between what is spoken and what is conveyed through body language. It would not be too strong to say the width of this gap represents mental health or the lack of it. A little disparity and there is irony, which has been called the song of the bird who has come to love his cage. This may well be an inevitable part of the human condition, following Winnicott's (1965) theory of the spectrum of true and false selves, but too much disparity between what is said and done and mental health is precarious. The received version of the story jars with the felt experience, and that way madness lies. The root conflict between what is felt and what is accepted as a descriptive narrative divides the self and makes it a battleground, to a greater or lesser degree. At its most extreme, it leads to suicide – or murder.

In the following chapter, 'It's not you, it's me: Oedipus was framed', I will go on to consider that cornerstone of psychoanalytic thinking, the Oedipus complex, in terms of the family set up. Britton (1989) has shown how the triangular relationship between parents and child opens ground for becoming aware of ourselves from other perspectives, for witnessing as well as experiencing, for the narrative of our lives. What can be included in this narrative, as I have suggested, influences the scope of what can be included in our sense of ourselves, and so lays the groundwork for our mental health. Beyond exclusion of disturbing elements from the narrative, there are also export/import opportunities in the parent-child relationship for intergenerationally unclaimed elements, that may disturb the parents' sense of themselves as only good and loving. We will look at the role this process plays in stories of suicidality and other severe mental health symptoms.

Psychoanalysis has much to teach about missing people and identity, and its core insights are largely substantiated by modern physiology and developmental research, though there is a significant shift of emphasis from the individual to the mutual construction of meaning. In 'Missing people: the presence of absence', I will revisit Freud's (1917) ideas about mourning and melancholia, or clinical depression, in physiological and developmental terms, asking what we do about missing what we cannot afford to miss, and what happens when we cannot acknowledge loss of vital supports we may never really have had.

In the next chapter, 'Getting your own back: revisiting resistance', I will explore the idea of resistance to change in an interdisciplinary light. Patients and families are sometimes described as 'hard-to-reach', a label that seems to locate the quality of disconnection in the client and not the worker. I will explore some implications of developmental research, which suggest that it is not that people consciously choose to continue to be trapped in an enactment of their painful childhood, far from it – it often makes them very isolated and unhappy. We are compelled to persist in what superficially seems like irrational behaviour for neurobiological reasons that I will try to describe, which mean an experienced relational truth gets re-presented. Human beings are intrinsically meaning-seeking, connection-seeking creatures. Embedded in the repetition can sometimes be a search, even if it feels like a defeated search, for a responsive other who can offer some kind of meaning. There is sometimes a hope that someone might finally really get the feeling of what has been going on, provided it paradoxically includes the feeling that nobody was/is there to get it. This in itself is potentially transformative, and is part of the long slow work of psychoanalytic psychotherapy.

The final chapter, 'It's not rocket science, it's neuroscience', considers some of the wider implications of twenty-first century development research for understanding mental health symptoms and thus for appropriate therapeutic response – implications we cannot afford to ignore. Much public money is invested in attempts to resolve seemingly intractable recurrent mental health problems. It may be that even with an unlimited budget, there could never be enough therapists working for long enough to make a difference to society's ills, given the need for long term relational cures for long term relationally formed mental health problems. However, taking into account the relational wiring of mind means that seeing symptoms as personal characteristics and focusing on the individual is not simply unjust but scientifically unsubstantiated and actually ineffective. Giving clinical consideration to family stories, and discovering the ghosts that may be lurking in the nursery (Fraiberg et al., 1975), may take the pathologizing out of mental health and generate a fuller understanding, which in itself helps regulation and recovery.

I will now turn to a consideration of the mediated and mediating nature of the perceptual system, a system that is very far from neutral, developing as it does in relation to what our experience has taught us to notice. This is the basis for a more relational approach to understanding the stories of our lives.

References

Bollas, C. (1987). *The Shadow of the Object: Psychoanalysis of the Unthought Known*. London: Free Association.

Britton, R. (1989). The missing link: Parental sexuality in the Oedipus complex. In R. Britton, M. Feldman, & E. O'Shaughnessy (Eds.), *The Oedipus Complex Today: Clinical Implications*. London: Karnac, 83.

Damasio, A. (1999). *The Feeling of What Happens: Body and Mind in the Making of Consciousness*. Florida: Harcourt.

Damasio, A. (2003). *Looking for Spinoza: Joy, Sorrow & the Feeling Brain*. London: Heinemann.

Eagleman, D. (2011). *Incognito*. New York: Random.

Eisold, K. (2010). *What You Don't Know You Know: Our Hidden Motives in Life, Business, and Everything Else*. New York: Other.

Ferguson, P. M. (2008). Social capital and children's wellbeing: A critical synthesis of the international social literature. *International Journal of Social Welfare*, 15:2–18.

Fraiberg, S., Adelson, E., & Shapiro, V. (1975). Ghosts in the Nursery: A psychoanalytic approach to the problems of impaired infant-mother relationships. *Journal of the American Academy of Child Psychiatry*, 14 (3):387–421.

Freud, S. (1917). Mourning and Melancholia. In J. Strachey (Ed.), *The Standard Edition of the Complete Psychological Works of Sigmund Freud*, Vol. 14:237–258. London: Hogarth.

Freud, S. (1930). Civilization and its discontents. In J. Strachey (Ed.), *The Standard Edition of the Complete Psychological Works of Sigmund Freud*, Vol. 21:57–146. London: Hogarth.

Ministry of Housing, Communities and Local Government (2011). *English indices of deprivation 2010*.Retrieved from https://www.gov.uk/government/statistics/english-indices-of-deprivation-2010

McGilchrist, I. (2009). *The Master and His Emissary: The Divided Brain and the Making of the Modern World*. New Haven: Yale.

Rizzolatti, G. & Craighero, L. (2004). The mirror-neuron system. *Annual Review of Neuroscience*, 27:169–192.

Schore, A. N. (1994). *Affect Regulation and the Origin of the Self: The Neurobiology of Emotional Development*. New York: Routledge.

Schwartz, J. M. (1999). A role for volition & attention in the generation of new brain circuitry. Towards a neurobiology of mental force. *Journal of Consciousness Studies*, 6(8–9):115–142.

Siegel, D. J. (1999). *The Developing Mind: Toward a Neurobiology of Interpersonal Experience.* New York: Guilford.

Solms, M. & Turnbull, O. (2002). *The Brain and the Inner World.* London: Karnac.

Winnicott, D. W. (1965). Ego distortion in terms of true and false self. In D. Winnicott (Ed.) *The Maturational Process and the Facilitating Environment: Studies in the Theory of Emotional Development*:140–157. New York: International Universities.

Winnicott, D. W. (1986). *Home Is Where We Start From: Essays by a Psychoanalyst.* New York: Norton.

Chapter 1

What you see is what you get

The nature of perception

A powerful truth is expressed in the old adage seeing is believing, but it is not the whole story. In this chapter, we will look at the nature of perception, and the 'evidence' of our eyes. It turns out to be much less straightforward and unequivocal than it sounds: what we see and how we see it are shaped by experience. Every possible level of perception is mediated by past experience; the very word 'recognition' means that it has been presented to our cognition before. We essentially allocate a meaning, out of our store of possible matches, before our conscious minds respond. Furthermore, we do not see new or conflicting perceptions once the received 'fact' is established in our minds and those of the people around us. No matter how extreme and omnipresent the evidence is, there is no limit to what the left brain (McGilchrist, 2009) will deny if it does not fit the received version. I hope to show how this process has implications for our sense of identity, and indeed for our mental and social health.

You may well have seen this picture of the impossible elephant, in which our eyes edit out the confusing legs:

Figure 1.1 The impossible elephant

The 'McGurk effect' (McGurk & MacDonald, 1976) is another visual trick, this time with sound effects. Type the phrase into a search engine, and you will see that a sound track is mismatched with a clip of someone talking. We hear one thing with our eyes open, another when they are closed. With our eyes open, visual perception cues tell us what we must be hearing; our hearing proves to be overruled by our eyes. What we take in from the world around us, what is present to our senses then, is not so much a presentation as a re-presentation, a post hoc rationalization. We are unconsciously working out what we could be hearing in the context of what we are seeing, which itself is influenced by what we have seen in the past. We know that the shape of the mouth cannot be making the sound, and so we do not hear it, but hear what would fit with the evidence of our eyes. In terms of perception, context is everything. Meaning, even in information so apparently undisputed as what we see with our own eyes, is not inherent. It is what we do with it that matters. And what we do with it is match it to previous experience (Ramachandran, 2012).

It turns out there is no such thing as immediate, that is, unmediated experience. Or rather, perhaps the absence of mediation constitutes what we see as madness. I will come back to this point later, in thinking about the link between trauma and mental health, but want to emphasize here that experience has to be mediated to make any kind of sense. It is clear from the impossible elephant and the mismatched sound clip that the sense it makes depends entirely on context.

In our earliest days, we use the mind of our caregiver, so often our mother, for context cues about meaning. We learn about what is acceptable, what can find expression in this relationship, through the emotional responses we read in her face and body. Later, we use the minds of others who matter to us in this way, as their emotional responses are reflected in their faces and body language. Once the early pattern is set, on the whole we use our own context-specific ways of understanding what happens to us – even, as we have seen, the 'evidence' of our own eyes. We discover through interacting with the world, in our particular socio-relational context, and past experience dictates what we perceive. The mind is excellent at filling in the gaps – for example, take peripheral vision. We have no perceptual cone cells for colour in our peripheral vision; instead we have rod cells there, which are good on picking up movement but unable to distinguish colour, and so what we should see is grayscale at the edges of our visual field. We do not; we see the colours we would expect things to be. Our perceptual system actually colours in the gaps, according to what we expect to find. Furthermore, we exclude contradictory evidence – like the actual sound in the McGurk effect experiment, or the actual shape of the impossible elephant.

The basis for this streamlining is the neuronal plasticity of the brain, a speciality of human evolution. We are born with very little pre-set 'software'. Instead we have the evolutionary advantage of being able to develop the processing we need to adapt to our specific environment, and so survive: belong, get protection, improve our chances of growing and flourishing. The more often we are exposed to a certain stimulus, the quicker we perceive it. This makes evolutionary sense; if you take too long to process information from your environment, you are at risk of being prey. The training effect of repeated exposure can be measured directly in the brain, which arrives at a result with less effort: functional Magnetic Resonance Imaging studies (Grotheer & Kovacs, 2014) show distinctly lower responses in processing areas when people are exposed to familiar environmental stimuli. It is particularly low in situations where we expect a very specific stimulus. This is efficient; we could not process everything from first principles and still function effectively. It also means we decide what we are seeing on the basis of what we have seen. Our past experiences, then, are essential in shaping our perception of the world and our relation to it, and this means that we tend to fit the experience to the template we already have. In the psychoanalytic world, this process is known as transference. Feelings and expectations from early relationships are transferred onto other people, particularly those who matter to us. Sensitive awareness of, and responsiveness to, this emotional information therefore constitute a central mechanism for therapeutic change, an idea I will explore in the final chapter.

Here though, I would like to look more closely at the neurobiology of transference. Siegel explains the cumulative exponential impact of this process:

> As representational processes anticipate experience, they also seek particular forms of interactions to match their expectations. In this way, the "bias" of a system leads it to perceive, process, and act in a particular manner. The outcome of this bias is to reinforce the very features creating the system's bias. As development evolves, the circuits involved become more differentiated and more elaborately engrained in an integrated system that continues to support its own characteristics.
>
> (1999:305)

This means that when the brain carries out a 'knowledge' or 'understanding' task, it actually manipulates representations, as it does in the sound clip, so that any idea that there is a direct correlation between what is there and what we actually hear is misguided. I have written elsewhere:

> Perceptual experience, then, is not just a function of what hits the eye, it is a function of the interrelationship between what comes in from the outside world and the central nervous system. The conclusion of a study of conscious and unconscious perception was that "perceptual processing itself is unconscious and automatically proceeds to all levels of analysis and redescription available to the perceiver" (Marcel, 1983:197). Marcel's findings cast doubt on the assumption that there is an equivalence between what we see and what is there; it is mediated.
>
> (Sutton, 2014:29)

Writing about perception, the neuroscientist Ramachandran writes, 'It's as if each of us is hallucinating all the time and what we call perception involves merely selecting the one hallucination that best matches current input' (2012:57). He stretches a point to stress the role of imaginative representation, and the link between past and present experience of all kinds. Take, for example, a sense as 'immediate' as taste, which is in fact not immediate but mediated. For example, Brochet (2001) studied wine tasting and found that taste is in fact a perceptive representation; red drops added to white wine made tasters use typically 'red' words like plum and raspberry to describe the smell and taste. In this study, Brochet argues that a type of cognitive coherence – we might just call it recognition – is necessary for the brain's processing of all sensory input, in order to prevent overload. Oddly, or perhaps not in terms of this chapter, experienced wine tasters' judgements have been found to be more influenced by colour than those of non-experienced wine tasters. The longer you've been doing something, the more likely you are to feel you know what you are doing. I have mentioned that Siegel (1999:30) describes the mind as an 'anticipation machine'. Out of the plethora of sensory information, we select the familiar – an interesting word: from the Latin for domestic, private, belonging to a family. We simply do not see the rest, or do not register it. In fact we delete from awareness any material that contradicts our familiar perspective, as studies of perception and consciousness (Lau & Rosenthal, 2011) have shown.

So although we can be all too sure of what we see, we cannot be sure what this very certainty may disguise – like the elephant we looked at earlier. Certainty blinds us to new possibilities; furthermore, we actively adapt what we see to what we expect: '[S]ubjective perception entails an ongoing reconstruction of the outside surroundings to an internal representation' (Salti et al., 2018:5). The same study sees conscious perception as a moment-to-moment updating process, which encompasses past perceptual events and adjusts the system for future, predicted ones. In this context, the information that is being processed is part of the subjective experience. If the adjusted account of the subjective experience, the story of what is happening for any one of us, broadly fits a new situation, there is no conflict. However, in clinical populations, the story does not fit the new environment and acts to isolate rather than to connect. Therapy can work to introduce the uninvited guest of what psychoanalysis calls countertransference – feelings that often belie the appearance. These emotional crosscurrents give us clues to what might really be going on 'below the surface' (Armstrong, 2004).

Essentially, this is how the therapist facilitates change. She (let's say) is guided by unexpected emotions understood as responses to unconscious expectations transferred upon her by the patient. I have written (Sutton, 2014) about how the implicit qualities of the relationship are transformed through a different response which, crucially, includes recognition of the old expectations, thus wiring in new relational possibilities for the anticipation machine of the mind to draw upon. I will examine the conflict inherent in this process in the chapter 'Getting your own back: revisiting resistance', which looks at the core psychoanalytic concept of resistance in the light of this human adaptation.

Here, however, it is clear from the above that what you see is not all you get – far from it; that would be like saying the boat sees the whole of the ocean. The question is, how to explore the ocean depths? In the psychoanalytic tradition, ideas about the undercurrents of transference and countertransference fed into Bick's (1964) thinking about observation. She alerted us fifty years ago to the fact that what we take in through our eyes acts as a depth charge, setting off waves of physical and emotional response in us. Modern neuroscience has supported this view. Siegel (1999), Schore (2012) and many others have shown how physiologically connected we are to other human beings, even when we are not in direct physical contact. There is an often underacknowledged undercurrent of felt experience, alongside the account of what can be seen.

The discovery of mirror neurons (Rizzolatti & Craighero, 2004) is particularly interesting here. We mentally put ourselves in another person's position, and actually feel the feelings ourselves – to the extent that we get sweaty palms when we see someone very high, for example, even on a screen. When we see someone stumble in the street, our mirror neurons fire as if we were about to fall. These neurons give us an experience of being in the other person's position; the feelings evoked by witnessing an action are the same as if we ourselves were in that position. This is the basis for empathy, for emotional connection. This discovery substantiates Freud's (1930) insight that boundaries between people can be blurred, but it puts the responsibility, the causal factor, in a different place. It is not individual pathology that creates the blurring, it is the emotional link between people facilitated by the mirror neuron, intrinsic to the human brain and common to everyday experience.

I will discuss the nature and function of these interesting neurons further shortly, but it is worth mentioning here that child development research into mother-infant micro-communication shows us their evolutionary, social, and cultural benefit. In the moment-by-moment world where relational life happens, babies are born ready to adapt to the environment in which they find themselves. They take moment-by-moment survival-dependent cues for meaning from the mother's face, to help them discover what they have to do to belong, as we see in frame-by-frame analysis of mothers' and babies' interactions (Beebe & Lachmann, 2002). Isolation is not an option for a newborn infant.

There is a parallel with therapy in these moment-by-moment interactions between mothers and babies, in that '[a]lthough the therapeutic medium is linguistic, the interactions we observe here and the patterns that emerge are largely implicit, in that much of what transpires does not enter reflective consciousness' (Boston Change Process Study Group, 2002:1053). It is the patterning process, the flow of interaction, that seems to forge the connection, rather than any specific content at declarative level. The mother's or therapist's face is a guide to the relational landscape, marking out safe territory and warning of danger zones.

Infancy research confirms the physiologically reciprocal nature of emotionality, and indeed thereby the co-construction of meaning. It becomes clear in the Beebe and Lachmann (2002) research, for example, that mothers are making themselves emotionally available to their babies in a way that helps the baby begin to make sense of what they are feeling. This is evident too in Tucker's (2006) work with parents and their infants, using filmed interactions to explore the parent's role in mirroring, marking, and meaning-making for the infant's developing sense of self.

External events, then, are understood through their emotional impact as mediated by the mind of an influential other (Bion, 1962), originally the mother – making her capacity for observational availability foundational to our understanding of ourselves. The Tavistock model of infant observation (Bick, 1964) is predicated on this understanding of the process of observation, involving reflecting on the waves of emotion experienced in observing a baby in their family as potential communication of states of mind/body happening in the baby and/or their family system. This model has since been used in organizational settings (Obholzer, 1987), and has been found to apply every bit as much to the waves of feeling evoked in the process of observing a case conference, or a board meeting. Reflections upon a process of observation that is three-dimensional rather than two, involving emotional depth as well as behavioural surface, can feed into understanding and transforming what goes on.

What we have to go on in a Tavistock-style observation is not just what is seen, however central that may seem. Alerted to our own blindness, and the nature of perception as part of the anticipation machine of the brain, this model of observation uses the resource of emotional undercurrents in the self, evoked by the context, and considered later from a number of perspectives in a group, as potential evidence for deeper undercurrents beneath the surface. This, in parallel with therapy with a disturbed child, or parent and infant, is a rich source of information about implicit ways of being in a particular group of people. The neurobiological basis for the intuition of undercurrents of feeling has become clearer since the discovery of mirror neurons.

Mirror neurons, countertransference, and role-responsiveness

The problem of identifying the deep and obscure current of what we feel indeed – as opposed to what we think we feel, or say we feel – has been central to the psychoanalytic project since its inception. Recent neuroscience has real bearing on this problem, highlighting as it does just how socially connected we are emotionally, how affected we are by the feelings of others. Iacoboni's (2009) innovative work on mirror neurons has established the neurobiological basis for the process of resonance, which links with the psychoanalytic notion of countertransference.

Mirror neurons are found to resonate with another's internal state through non-verbal signals like eye contact, tone of voice, posture, gestures, and the timing and intensity of speech. This information is relayed in a kind of whole-body empathy circuit downward from the cortex to the limbic system, which processes emotion, then lower still to the brainstem and the body. Actual physiological changes occur in the presence of another person in response to their emotional state: heart rate changes, intestines churn, lungs expand and contract, muscles tighten – and these shifts in our inner bodily states travel back upward to the right prefrontal cortex, where we gain awareness of our body's internal state. Freud's idea of badly drawn boundaries seems relevant here. Who is to say whose feelings are whose?

Sandler's concept of role-responsiveness may shed some light. Talking about psychoanalysis, he suggests that parallel to the 'free-floating attention' of the analyst 'is what I should like to call his free-floating responsiveness' (Sandler, 1976:45). He goes on to say, presciently, that it 'seems that a complicated system of unconscious cues, both given and received, is involved' (Sandler, 1976:47). Sandler's ideas suggest a transitional area between worlds in which a role relationship is evoked. Such evocations are crucial to the understanding of a limiting world view. The evoked role relationship – I mentioned earlier that psychoanalysts call this process transference, in which qualities of earlier relationships are transferred to the therapy relationship – is itself the basis for connection between that world view and a new perspective, and begins to create the path from one to the other. It is only when you notice the path you are on that you can change direction – after all, the unconscious bias that Siegel (1999) alerts us to leads us to perceive, process, and act in a way that reinforces that very bias.

Seeing, being, and identity: the formative nature of observation

Having thought about the surprisingly filtered nature of perception, let us look now at how this relates to our sense of self. As babies, our pre-reflective gaze takes in from our environment implicit signals of ways of being in the world. The idea I would like to explore here is that in learning how to be, through observation in its fullest sense, taking into account the undercurrents, the baby learns who to be. Implicitly, ways of being are countenanced or not countenanced. Even the verb 'to countenance' suggests an available face. Its opposite, an unavailable face, as still face experiments (Tronick et al., 1975) show, is disturbing for the baby – who soon learns what behaviour can be faced, just as we do in a new social situation. The newcomer, then, learns how to be in this particular group through observation.

Essentially, observation is formative: both what we see and how we are seen – consequently, how we see ourselves in that social relational context – forms the basis for identity, in work and social settings every bit as much as in family groups.

Stern (1985), among others, has established that in learning how to be, through this process of emotionally informed observation, the baby learns who to be. Stern talks about 'ways-of-being-with' as shaping forces, and suggests of the observed infant that it is 'the actual shape of interpersonal reality, specified by the interpersonal variants that really exist, that helps determine the developmental course' (Stern, 1985:255).

In thinking about the formative nature of observation, it is worth a quick foray into quantum mechanics and Heisenberg's (1930) uncertainty principle, which holds that the act of observing a quantum particle will in some way affect its behaviour, at least as far as that behaviour is knowable. In quantum physics, as in poetry, the link is made between observer and observed. The Copenhagen interpretation of quantum mechanics, which, interestingly, arose out of a dialogue between the physicist Bohr and his student Heisenberg in the 1920s, holds that a quantum particle does not exist in one state or another, but potentially in all of its possible states at once. It is only when we observe its state that the set of probabilities immediately and randomly assumes only one of the possible values, and that is the state we observe. A similar view emerges from the practice of art. Klee (1918/2013) wrote, 'Art does not reproduce the visible; rather, it makes visible'. From these very different viewpoints, things come into being, form an identity, through being seen. An example of this principle happened at a gallery in Lisbon, when two people entered a room in which a film had just finished, and the credits were rolling. 'It's just names', they agreed rather sadly, and left. They were both right and wrong. In the particle/moment they observed, they were right to observe just names, but had they stayed, they would have seen the wave, the context, the overall pattern of Araujo's (2015) film, *Mulheres d'Apolo*.

Child psychotherapists undertake a two-year weekly observation of a baby as part of their training in order to help them 'conceive vividly' (Bick, 1964:558) a fuller sense of the wave of infantile experience than the particle or brief snapshot any one meeting could provide. Other trainings have followed suit. The use of the verb 'conceive' is important here. It links with Bion's (1962) ideas about conception and pre-conception in relation to thinking, implying a vital, embodied kind of process in which thoughts are brought into being, and thus can become the basis for a lively connection, with other thoughts and connections in the same mind, or in another. Thomson Salo's (2014) work with parents and infants is informed by neurobiology, attachment theory and developmental psychology as well as Winnicott's (1965) thinking. She establishes the possibility of a new kind of relating through observing and reflecting upon what might be in the baby's mind, thus representing the baby to the parents in a way that helps them see their baby differently. This in turn shapes the baby's sense of himself, and helps develop his own reflective capacity. The process opens the way for new connections and conceptions, a new identity.

How the baby is seen to be is who she feels herself to be, and how she identifies herself – even if there are sad, uncomfortable, unacknowledged undercurrents that do not fit the picture. Panksepp and Solms (2012) suggest three levels of emotional processing, the first conscious, in which emotional action networks in the brain generate states that feel good or bad – effects with an evolutionary value in promoting survival and reproductive success. They see the second level as involving associative learning and memory in the context of a particular way of living. The third level is descriptive. 'Analysis of the declarative tertiary processes in relation to these deeper layers also reveals the remarkable extent to which introspective awareness distorts the underlying causal events' (2012:2). There is thus emotion which feels good or bad, there is learning by unconscious association, and there is the capacity for any amount of stretch and distortion in the account of it.

Herein lies the potential force of disparity between the story of what happens and the felt experience. At all three levels, from what feels good or bad, learning and memory assigned to a particular environmental space and time, and introspective awareness we can declare, parental influence is a directive factor. One implication of this for all of us as babies is that to all intents and purposes, the parental account of each of us, until someone sees us differently, is how we see ourselves, even if there has been any amount of distortion. A young girl, say, is seen by her disturbed mother as monstrous, and begins to inhabit the identification, behaving in more and more monstrous ways. In order to belong, she needs to get with the programme and be a monster. Especially if her mother is unreliably available, she cannot afford to distance herself from her mother's view, even though it is at huge cost to herself. The alternative may seem to her to be to get rid of herself, and that may well be one way she finds of coping with her distress in adolescence. In essence, in that putative suicide attempt, she is impersonating her mother's response to the child she sees. This itself may be a transferred part of her mother's own child self that was in turn felt to be unacceptable to her grandmother. I will return to consider stories of suicidality involving such tortuously entangled identities in the chapters, 'It's not you, it's me: Oedipus was framed' and 'Missing people: the presence of absence'.

Meanwhile, if, as Damasio says, the human mind is the idea of the human body, and 'mental processes are grounded in the brain's mappings of the body, collections of neural patterns that portray responses to events that cause emotions and feelings' (2003:12), then whose idea of whose body holds sway? The child development research into very early formative interactions would suggest that it is the mother's idea of the baby's body that forms the basis for the child's idea of his or her bodily self.

The wisdom of Fraiberg et al.'s (1975) seminal paper, *Ghosts in the Nursery*, and other work on the intergenerational transmission of trauma (see Fromm, 2012) would suggest that a mother's idea of her baby's body will be unconsciously influenced by her own experience of herself in infancy, inevitably taking in her own parents' experience of her, with all that that involved. Tucker's (2006) work shows how damaging this identification process can be when it goes wrong, resulting in a disordered sense of self, and potential lifelong disadvantage. The intervention Tucker and her colleagues in a parent-infant partnership service offer is another mind, another experience of being taken in, a different framing relationship (Sutton, 2014) for both mother and baby, resulting in the possibility of a new idea of the baby's physical and emotional self. In Bion's terms, the potentiality of a preconception needs to meet with a conception to make a realization of a new way of being. More prosaically, that the single most significant factor in success at school is teacher expectation speaks volumes about this. Research (Rosenthal & Jacobson, 1968) shows how children live up or down to teachers' ideas of their potential.

Psychoanalytic thinking illuminates what happens when emotional undercurrents that do not fit the received narrative cannot be observed or acknowledged. Steiner (1985) has written powerfully about work with very ill mental health patients, which also elucidates mechanisms encountered in the everyday world. He describes the notion of turning a blind eye, an important way of permitting retreat from reality by both acknowledging and disavowing of the truth of an experience. For example, in the case of OCD, there are often symptoms which express a feeling of unsafety through its opposite, the urge to check and to lock. Steiner's avowal and disavowal are in evidence here: the clue is in the symptom. Since minds are wired relationally (Schore, 1994; Balbernie, 2001), we are led to assume that the disavowed material is not acceptable in the primary relationship. To the extent that the person concerned identifies with the feeling of unsafety, he or she is not acceptable in the primary relationship. Outside this is a very unsafe place to be for a young child. The person with OCD is caught between a rock and a hard place, without hope of somewhere safe. The symptom can thus be understood as a silent call for help which is both part and not part of the person's identity. It is not that the truth has altogether disappeared from awareness; indeed it is implicit in the means taken to avoid it – somebody is not safe – but it feels impossible to act upon it. This is also accurate; it has already happened. Steiner (1985) suggests that the way forward is to acknowledge the impossibility, the trap, to step into the world of the patient and walk a mile in the shoes of their internalized parent, taking responsibility for what is inflicted in the transference relationship, so that a representation of that finally finds expression. The difficult feeling, lack of safety, say, is acknowledged in the relationship with the analyst. The patient can then come to know it differently, and eventually identify with it, or more specifically, identify with the analyst's own non-rejecting relation to the possibility of it. It has the feeling then of a potentiality, not a determining characteristic.

It will be apparent that I am making a connection between invisible emotional undercurrents and what are felt to be disavowed parts of the self. In the child psychotherapy tradition, Music, writing on executive function in work with an individual child, says: 'My attention was holding him together, a first phase on the way to his own attention doing this' (2014:10). The task seems to be one of finding a relation between attributed internalized qualities felt to be different parts of the self, some unacknowledged but making their presence felt all the more intensely for that.

There is a parallel with everyday group process. Walker (2005) writes about observing a group in a school, and attending to the different parts of group identity distributed among them. Her title question, *Who will be the naughty one now?* arose when a member of their group was absent for the day, and seems to me to encapsulate neatly the role-responsiveness in the organization in the mind (Armstrong, 2005) of the children. There needs to be a 'naughty one', and the role is soon assigned. The child who picks up the role is likely to feel troubled but unsure why; it is my own clinical experience that children in this position may well attribute the troubled feeling to their own badness. There is then the opposite of a symbiotic relationship between the vacant role in the group and the sense of self of the child who volunteers/is volunteered. This might be an example of the distinction Bollas (1989) makes between fate and destiny, in which fate seems to be a blindly inevitable consequence of the way you are seen in the world you are in and the role you accept or even seek, while destiny is a working out of something more idiosyncratic and creative, finding a relation other than compliance to the dictates of your fate. The troubled feeling of the re-assigned 'naughty one' might lead in either direction, depending on the sense she makes of her frustration and distress. She is helped in this task through being observed by a mind available to her distress and the range of potential meanings for it.

Schimmenti (2012) highlights the link between the lack of this responsive connection and shame. He sees shame as arising from many sources, but being essentially a relational experience, and at its most pathological, the result of neglect or abuse. The cycle of rupture and repair is a key factor in regulating this debilitating emotion (Schore, 1998). The lack of psychobiological regulation leads to unpredictable outbursts, exacerbating feelings of shame and exposure, grounded in a fear of rejection or humiliation in the eyes of a critical other.

Public sector culture in the UK today suffers from what Rustin (2004) calls 'the pervasive systems of audit and inspection which now plague every inch of the public sector', which present the shame-inducing sense of an unavailable, potentially critical other. Pathological organizing, both internal and external, can be a defence against a world in which there seems to be no real curiosity about causes, or awareness of a wider context, just narrow critical scrutiny in pursuit of less and less realistic targets. The outside perspective is necessary for growth and learning, but it is potentially experienced as critical – especially if it is coming from an authority figure interested in outcomes but not causes, the what and not the how.

There is thus the problem of what happens when emotional undercurrents are made visible, in creative tension with the problem of what happens when they are not. It is a complex matter, calling for a delicate response. Observational skills such as those nurtured and developed in Bick's (1964) training are crucial, it seems to me, in offering a space for reflection in which emotional undercurrents deleted from the received account can be brought into awareness. Unconscious expectations are thereby examined, while suspending the notion of blame, thereby encouraging the kind of getting to know that is all we can apprehend of reality.

The shaping quality of attention

The mutually responsive connection in the primary relationship between parent and child is crucial then in making sense of emotional communications. There follows from the neuroscience I have touched on above an apprehension of the mediating filter of the sensory/mind/brain system and therefore the intersubjectively formative nature of observation. In the experience both of seeing and of being seen, we learn how/who to be, formatively in our families, and then later, too, in social and work settings.

However, when the focus is on the explicit, the surface of things, it cannot address the implicit, the flow of undercurrents, which as we have seen is how most human learning happens. It seems that the public sector inspection culture so prevalent today operates in this way, leaving out vital information and distorting the picture in the way that Panksepp and Solms (2012) illuminate. In fact McGilchrist (2009) warns that western civilization operates in just this way, prioritizing the particular emphasis in the awareness of the left brain, the hemisphere of what, over the right hemisphere of how, in a misleading and dangerous imbalance.

The practice of emotionally-informed observation described above, initiated by Bick and increasingly used in organizations, as well as in family work, guards against this misrepresentation. Sprince (2009), a child psychotherapist, describes a complex and challenging situation she met with in consulting to a local authority home for children. She tells the story of the elephant, in which each blind witness feels a different part and comes to a different conclusion about the identity of the thing in question – a snake, a wall, a silk fan, and so on. She describes calling a network meeting, to facilitate a conversation that could incorporate a fuller range of perspectives, a more open-ended pooling of knowledge, so that between them, they could be aware of all the parts of the elephant, and see it as a whole.

We need another observational experience, being seen and thus seeing differently, through the perspective of someone outside the frame, if we are to learn new things, and incorporate, as Eisold (2010) puts it, 'what you don't know you know'. Sprince was in a position – that is, an observational position in a liminal place between the organization and the outside world – to call a meeting and offer this potential view of a fuller range of experience. However, from the ideas explored above, it would seem that this view will facilitate change to the extent that we are able to identify with it rather than defend against it.

Steiner's (1993) work on psychic retreats, and Rosenfeld's (1971) thinking about the gang state of mind, illuminate the difficulty of leaving an organization, internal or external, after an allegiance has been forged. I think something of this state of mind is apparent in all kinds of contexts, at work and at home. Giving up the safety and protection of some kind of organization involves acknowledging and facing the pain and vulnerability that led to the need for it in the first place. It involves loss of certainty, which inevitably induces anxiety. Perhaps it is not so much that the unknown in itself brings anxiety, but rather the intrinsic possibility that things will go wrong, and that we may be unprepared and unprotected – better the devil we know.

Furthermore, exposing to view the muddle and uncertainty of unpreparedness evokes feelings of shame, humiliation, and embarrassment. Mitigating the primitive feeling of shame is a sense of someone alongside who can see the mess and feel sympathy rather than disgust or contempt; furthermore, can see beyond it to the possibility of something new emerging. My contention is that this sense of someone alongside, as well as seeing from outside, is facilitated by observation as Bick conceived it, involving a broader, more empathic, right brain awareness, in connection with a selective left brain, pattern-sensing awareness (McGilchrist, 2009).

Like co-operating parents, this offers a model of thinking that is open to emotional undercurrents, but not at the expense of an external perspective. Even the result of this process is not final and summative; like a snapshot of now, it does not encompass the flow and the possibility of change. However, the process of arriving at it forms a bridge between the anticipation machine and the world outside, in which other ways of seeing and being are possible. Like Heisenberg's uncertainty principle, in order to apprehend the truth, you need a dialogue between the particle and the wave, between how things are in this particular moment, pattern or constellation – 'just names', for example – and the flow of emotional experience – the film of the dance. The challenge for the therapist, indeed for all of us when we are trying to change, is to pay attention to this dialogue, including the essential information of the feeling of what happens (Damasio, 1999), in the face of external pressures. Needless to say, this can only ever be a work in progress.

If observation is formative, then, in its capacity to take in implicit emotional experience, it is potentially transformative. What we see is not all we get; what we feel is taken in too, and can be taken into account, if someone is there to witness and respond to it. I will look in the final chapter of this book at how connections are made when there has been dissonance or distortion between the account and the felt experience. Here though, I will turn next to consider the significance for our mental health of the relationship between what is communicated, and how it is received.

References

Araujo, V. (2015). *Mulheres d'Apolo. Video. Shown as Part of Tension and Freedom.* Lisbon: Modern Art Center, Gulbenkian Foundation. Retrieved from https://loop-barcelona.com/videocloop/video/apollos-women-mulheres-de-apollo/.

Armstrong, D. (2004). Emotions in organizations: Disturbances or intelligence? In C. Huffington, D. Armstrong, W. Halton, L. Hoyle, & J. Pooley (Eds.), *Working below the Surface: The Emotional Life of Contemporary Organizations*:127–150. London: Karnac.

Armstrong, D. (2005). R. French (Ed.), *Organization in the Mind: Psychoanalysis, Group Relations and Organizational Consultancy.* London: Karnac.

Balbernie, R. (2001). Circuits and circumstances: The neurobiological consequences of early relationship experiences and how they shape later behaviour. *Journal of Child Psychotherapy*, 27(3):237–255.

Beebe, B. & Lachmann, F. (2002). *Infant Research and Adult Treatment: Co-constructing Interactions.* London: Analytic.

Bick, E. (1964). *Notes on Infant Observation in Psycho-Analytic Training*. In A. Briggs (Ed.), *(2002) Surviving Space*. London: Karnac.
Bion, W. R. (1962). *Learning from Experience*. London: Heinemann.
Bollas, C. (1989). *Forces of Destiny: Psychoanalysis and Human Idiom*. New Jersey: Aronson.
Brochet, F. (2001). *Tasting: Chemical Object Representation in the Field of Consciousness*. Application presented for the grand prix of the Académie Amorim following work carried out towards a doctorate from the Faculty of Oenology, University of Bordeaux. Retrieved from web.archive.org/web/20070928231853/www.academie-amorim.com/us/laureat_2001/brochet.pdf.
Boston Change Study Process Group, Bruschweiler-Stern, N. Harrison, A. M., Lyons-Ruth, K., Morgan, A. C., Nahum, J. P., Sander, L. W., Stern, D. N., & Tronick, E. Z. (2002). Explicating the implicit: The local level and the microprocess of change in the analytic situation. *International Journal of Psychoanalysis*, 83(5):1051–1062.
Damasio, A. (1999). *The Feeling of What Happens: Body and Mind in the Making of Consciousness*. Florida: Harcourt.
Damasio, A. (2003). *Looking for Spinoza: Joy, Sorrow & the Feeling Brain*. London: Heinemann.
Eagleman, D. (2011). *Incognito*. New York: Random.
Eisold, K. (2010). *What You Don't Know You Know: Our Hidden Motives in Life, Business, and Everything Else*. New York: Other.
Fraiberg, S., Adelson, E. & Vivian Shapiro, V. (1975). Ghosts in the nursery: A psychoanalytic approach to the problems of impaired infant-mother relationships. *Journal of the American Academy of Child Psychiatry*, 14 (3):387–421.
Freud, S. (1930). Civilization and its Discontents. In J. Riviere (Trans.), *The Standard Edition of the Complete Psychological Works of Sigmund Freud*, Vol. 21:57–146. London: Hogarth.
Fromm, M. G. (Ed.). (2012). *Lost in Transmission: Studies of Trauma across Generations*. London: Karnac.
Grotheer, M. & Kovacs, G. (2014). Repetition probability effects depend on prior experiences. *Journal of Neuroscience*, 34(19):6640–6646.
Heisenberg, W. (1930). In C. Eckhart & F. C. Hoyt (Trans.), *The Physical Principles of Quantum Theory*. Chicago: University of Chicago.
Iacoboni, M. (2009). Imitation, empathy & mirror neurons. *Annual Review of Psychology*, 60:653–670.
Klee, P. (2013). *Creative Confession*. London: Tate. (Original work published 1918).
Lau, H. & Rosenthal, D. (2011). Empirical support for higher-order theories of conscious awareness. *Trends in Cognitive Sciences*, 15(8). Retrieved from www.summer12.isc.uqam.ca/page/docs/readings/Lau-Hakwan/Lau-Rosenthal-Empirical-support-for-higher-order-theories-of-conscious-awareness.pdf.

Marcel, A.J. (1983). Conscious and unconscious perception: experiments on visual masking and word recognition. *Cognitive Psychology*, 15(2): 197–237.

McGilchrist, I. (2009). *The Master and His Emissary: The Divided Brain and the Making of the Modern World*. New Haven: Yale.

McGurk, H. & MacDonald, J. (1976). Hearing lips and seeing voices. *Nature*, 264:746–748.

Music, G. (2014). Top Down and Bottom Up: Trauma, executive functioning, emotional regulation, the brain and child psychotherapy. *Journal of Child Psychotherapy*, 40(1):3–19.

Obholzer, A. (1987). Institutional dynamics and resistance to change. *Psychoanalytic Psychotherapy*, 2(3):201–206.

Panksepp, J. & Solms, M. (2012). What is neuropsychoanalysis? Clinically relevant studies of the minded brain. *Trends in Cognitive Sciences*, 16(1):6–8.

Ramachandran, V. S. (2012). *The Tell-Tale Brain: Unlocking the Mystery of Human Nature*. London: Random.

Rizzolatti, G. & Craighero, L. (2004). The mirror-neuron system. *Annual Review of Neuroscience*, 27:169–192.

Rosenfeld, H. (1971). A clinical approach to the psychoanalytic theory of the life and death instincts: An investigation into the aggressive aspects of narcissism. *International Journal of Psycho-Analysis*, 52:69–178.

Rosenthal, R. & Jacobson, L. (1968). Teacher expectations for the disadvantaged. *Scientific American*, 218:4.

Rustin, M.J. (2004). Rethinking audit and inspection. *Soundings*, 26:86–107.

Salti, M., Harel, A. & Marti, S. (2018). Conscious perception: Time for an update? *Cognitive Neuroscience*, 21:1–7.

Sandler, J. (1976). Countertransference and role-responsiveness. *International Review of Psycho-Analysis*, 3:43–47.

Schimmenti, A. (2012). Unveiling the hidden self: Developmental trauma and pathological shame. *Psychodynamic Practice: Individuals, Groups & Organizations*, 18(2):195–211.

Schore, A.N. (1994). *Affect Regulation and the Origin of the Self: The Neurobiology of Emotional Development*. New Jersey: Erlbaum.

Schore, A.N. (1998). Early shame experiences & the development of the infant brain. In Gilbert, P. & Andrews, B. (Eds.), *Shame: Interpersonal Behaviour, Psychopathology & Culture*: 57–77. London: Oxford University.

Schore, A.N. (2012). *The Science of the Art of Psychotherapy*. New York: Norton.

Siegel, D. J. (1999). *The Developing Mind: Toward a Neurobiology of Interpersonal Experience*. New York: Guilford.

Sprince, J. (2009). Working with complex systems and networks around looked after children and young people. Retrieved from www.nice.org.uk/guidance/ph28/resources/looked-after-children-ep11-working-with-complex-systems-jenny-sprince2.

Steiner, J. (1985). Turning a blind eye: The cover up for Oedipus. *International Review of Psychoanalysis*, 12:161–172.

Steiner, J. (1993). *Psychic Retreats: Pathological Organisations in Psychotic, Neurotic and Borderline Patients*. London: Routledge.

Stern, D. (1985). *The Interpersonal World of the Infant: A View from Psychoanalysis and Developmental Psychology*. New York: Basic.

Sutton, S. (2014). *Being Taken In: The Framing Relationship*. London: Karnac.

Thomson Salo, F. (2014). *Infant Observation: Creating Transformative Relationships*. London: Karnac.

Tronick, E., Adamson, L.B., Als, H., & Brazelton, T.B. (1975). *Infant emotions in normal and pertubated interactions*. Presentation at the biennial meeting of the Society for Research in Child Development, Denver, CO.

Tucker, J. (2006). Using video to enhance the learning in a first attempt at 'Watch, Wait and Wonder'. *Infant Observation: International Journal of Infant Observation & Its Applications*, 9(2):125–138.

Walker, G. (2005). 'Who will be the naughty one now?' Using observational skills in work with primary aged children in a small school-based group. *Infant Observation: International Journal of Infant Observation & Its Applications*, 8(1):19–31.

Winnicott, D. W. (1965). *The Maturational Process and the Facilitating Environment: Studies in the Theory of Emotional Development*. New York: International Universities.

Chapter 2

Behaviour as communication

Do you get me?

Leading on from the distinction between what we see and what we get, this chapter explores the function of behaviour as communication, and the potential gap between what is spoken and what is conveyed through body language. It would not be too strong to say the width of the gap between what is experienced and what can be spoken represents mental health or the lack of it. Freud (1897) suggests that we suffer from unclaimed relational reminiscences. This may well be an inevitable part of the human condition; we cannot speak all that we feel. Too much disparity between what is said and done, though, and mental health is precarious. The received version of the story jars with the felt experience, and that way madness lies. I will try to show how conflict between what is felt and what is accepted as the story of what happens divides the self and makes it a battleground, to a greater or lesser degree. At its most extreme, it leads to suicide – or murder: it's her/him or me. We will look more closely at the roots of that disturbing conflict in the next chapter, 'It's not you, it's me: Oedipus was framed'.

Here we will look at how behaviour communicates states of mind. This truth sounds self-evident. Maybe we assume that disturbed behaviour arises from disturbed states of mind, but perhaps there has been less focus on the fact that it not only reflects disturbance but conveys it. Communication, when it works, is not just broadcasting; it involves someone else on the receiving end. A play needs an audience, and stands or falls by the audience's response. Schutz highlights the adaptive function of emotionality, which serves as 'the right brain's "red phone", compelling the mind to handle urgent matters without delay' (2005:15). The red phone can only convey urgent news if someone picks up immediately to hear it, and, crucially, to respond. What if the red phone rings, and no one picks up? Or someone picks up, and triggers World War III? Or says there is nothing the matter? In thinking about the communicative power of body language, we need to consider the state of mind of the transmitter, and also the state of mind of the receiver. This interrelation shapes how the communication is understood, and what happens next.

It takes a surprising degree of sensitivity on the part of another mind to receive a behavioural communication. It is a quietly miraculous, extraordinarily complex process, happening every day. Trevarthen (2005) highlights the evidence from brain imaging research that the human brain can match action, regulation, emotion, intention, and ways of moving with corresponding events in others' minds. We know from infancy research that mind-to-mind improvisation, mediated by emotions carried by the sight, sound and feel of human bodies moving, is in a baby from birth. There is evidence (Kisilevsky et al., 2009) that the baby's brain begins learning in utero to improve the chances of a good connection with the mother, picking up her voice and speech patterns from before birth. The baby is predisposed to relate, ready to meet Braten's (1992) 'virtual other'. He evokes a partner's response from the very first moments of life, through imitations and vocal phrases that invite connection. When things go well, the improvisation of a mutual musical story arises between the baby's mind and body and the subtly attuned responses of the other; a 'protoconversation', like a duet (Trevarthen, 2005). Through an emotionally resonant connection we feel the music of what happens; it resonates through the musical qualities of vocal and behavioural sequences, like tone, timing, pitch, rhythm, and pace. Mirror neurons in our brain light up and play the same emotional music they would play if we were in the other person's shoes. A kind of dance between partners emerges, which can be more or less attuned and harmonious. The harmony is achieved not so much through the content as through the mutuality of the partnership – the sympathy of feelings implicit in each partner's readiness to relate, their openness to how it feels for the other, and how it feels between them. Like the sweetness of sugar, the emotional qualities of the connection are not stored in any one part(ner), but arise between them, in the moment.

Mental health symptoms arise through failures of this connection, when missteps in the dance are not repaired, and may not even be acknowledged. Such symptoms are rooted in pain that cannot be transmitted, because someone is not ready and waiting to receive the communication, sometimes because they are preoccupied with their own unacknowledged pain. Again and again, Schutz's (2005) red phone rings, initially in hope of someone to receive the call, but as the silence continues to deafen, it rings to show how nobody ever listens. In order to achieve a connection in future, one half of the duet will now need to convey what it feels like when nobody responds. We will come back to this poignant and frustrating misconnection in the chapter, 'Getting your own back, revisiting resistance', but suffice it to say here that in order to re-establish connection in these circumstances, someone needs to show they understand that nobody's there to hear you. If we think of the red phone ringing in vain as a symptom, a call for help that paradoxically needs to be witnessed as going unanswered, it reflects the truth of someone's relational experience, especially when it has been traumatic. It is ringing to show how no one picks up; it is an attempt at connection designed to evade connection. Connection, in this context, is not the point. Here we have the conundrum at the heart of therapeutic practice that causes so much anguish, to therapists as well as their patients. We need a witness to the unheard call, someone to take compassionate responsibility for not answering, before we can let ourselves be heard.

Trauma is held as an embodied memory, an experienced truth that is unrepresented, unrepresentable in fact, in the context of someone's life, other than by the symptom. What looks like madness can be understood as a symptom in search of meaning, which has yet to be taken in by another mind. A traumatic experience is lodged in the body at a non-verbal level, and cannot be approached or expressed through words, but only through behaviour, or body language, which tells the story of our lives – if someone is there to hear it.

In the previous chapter, we saw how what we notice and how we respond is experience-dependent. Children learn to regulate their behaviour by anticipating their caregivers' responses to them. Researchers (Beebe & Lachmann, 2002) have filmed and analyzed rapid and subtle interactions between babies and their carers, and found patterns of relating emerging by the microsecond. There were remarkably beautiful moments in attuned partnerships, such as both faces rising in harmony into glorious smiles. There were disturbing moments, too, such as anger or disgust showing plainly for a fraction of a second on a mother's face, and infants becoming frantically distressed or frozen. In some mother-infant partnerships, a 'chase and dodge' pattern emerged, in which the mother chased her baby's attention as the baby turned away. Beebe and Lachmann (2002) found of these partnerships that rather than tuning out, the baby was in fact acutely vigilant, exquisitely sensitive to the mother's every movement.

These children turned out to have an insecure attachment pattern at eighteen months.

Through the particular call and response patterns then between each tiny child and their parents, internal working models (Bowlby, 1969) are constructed. A child's internal working models are defined not just by what goes on in these patterning relationships, but importantly, how they feel. The brain develops through these very patterns, internalizing a way of being in the world. So we adapt to our own social context, which becomes a working model for future relating. As we have seen, this shapes our awareness. Furthermore, we delete what does not fit the story we are sticking to. If the deleted material is not too important, it may never need to find expression. If there is a crucial misfit between Damasio's (1999) feeling of what happens and the received version of the story however, our bodies give us away. In *Theatres of the Body*, McDougall (1989) suggests that the body has its own way of knowing and expressing experiences; it expresses what the mind cannot bear.

Increasingly, research suggests that the body of the child expresses what the parent's mind cannot bear. In writing about parental bereavement, Goldsmith and Cowen (2011:189) describe how the infant's body becomes 'the vehicle for expressing unresolved trauma as a consequence of devastating loss in the mother'. They explain how, after a series of terminations and then miscarriages, a mother could not see her baby as she was, and try to understand what her screaming might be communicating – there was too much in the way. She was already occupied by deep pain for the loss of babies she had not carried to term, and thus felt she already knew what her baby's screaming meant: it was a punishment. The baby's grandmother agreed, with some *schadenfreude*, claiming it was her revenge on her daughter, who had herself screamed as a baby. A mutually open responsive connection between this mother and her baby is precluded by untransmitted emotional pain, which occupies the body and continually seeks re-presentation. The sweet improvisation cannot happen between them; the part available to the child in the drama of connection is already written.

In more everyday ways, too, a parent can struggle to be available to process their child's emotion when their own is very strong. Zalidis (2009), a doctor working in general practice, explores the emotions behind physical symptoms. He writes of a child with an exaggerated, fixed smile presenting with a symptom of eyes misting over. Influenced by the idea of the mind's eye, the link between eyes and emotion, he asked the child whether she had been crying recently. It emerged that her mother had been crying recently, as Anna's father had left home. Her mother was getting help for her emotional state, but she reported that Anna was coping very well on her own. Anna's symptom, however, begged the question. It expressed the sadness in her that her mother could not, at that time, bear to know about.

I mentioned earlier Steiner's (1985) use of the notion of turning a blind eye, which is a way of permitting retreat from unacceptable reality by both acknowledging and disavowing it. It is not that an unacceptable truth has altogether disappeared from awareness, indeed it is implicit in the means taken to avoid it; but it feels impossible to act upon it, or even comment upon it. However, Steiner does not focus on the relational roots of the feeling of unacceptability. Whose blind eye is turned? The logic of the infancy research discussed above would suggest that the blind eye is internalized from the unseeing eye of a partner who was not available for connection, a preoccupied state of mind in the primary framing relationship (Sutton, 2014). The turning away would seem to offer essential protection from knowledge that would destroy the survival pact with the primary caregiver, the story the caregiver can bear.

My sense is that in Steiner's (1993) psychic retreat, the troubled, perhaps traumatized mind is retreating from the constant struggle between self and other, as an army retreats from battle. There is a need for a resting place, midway between the two possibilities that seem to be available in traumatic relationships: destruction of the self in favour of the object, or destruction of the object in favour of the survival of the self.

The assumptions driving this appalling apprehension seem to arise from unmediated extreme experience. In a post-traumatic state, bad feelings dominate and inhabit the body. There is no sense that they will ever go away; there is instead a feeling that time stops. The person feels they are trapped in a permanent terrifying present, rather than that they are experiencing a contingent, understandable, temporary response. Without a mediating mind, which uses feelings as cues to attend to the meaning of what might be going on, there is no way of finding a relation to trauma. It simply invades and is felt to be present. It is a state of body, and not a state of mind, and precipitates the body into flight, fight, or freeze reactions. This makes people prone to overreact as if in serious danger and even intimidate others in response to what seem to be minor provocations (van der

Kolk & Ducey, 1989). The sense that they have been intimidating can then itself be shame-inducing, reinforcing a feeling of responsibility, of being the source of badness or of having it located in them by others.

Anxiety disorders, chronic hyperarousal, and behavioural disturbances are regularly described in traumatized children. These behavioural responses are sometimes attributed to the individual, as a personal characteristic – even though animal experiments (Suomi, 1984) have shown that all primates subjected to early abuse and deprivation show disturbance in relationships throughout life. If an attribution of disturbance as a personal characteristic of the individual child is made by someone important to the child, it is incorporated into his or her sense of self, exacerbating the damage. The feeling is not that something bad has happened to me; I am something bad. Yet in fact, the field trials for the 4th edition of the American Psychiatric Association's Diagnostic and Statistical Manual of Mental Disorders (DSM) showed that these symptoms are not an individual property of the child, but tend to occur together in response to trauma. The severity of the symptoms is proportional to the age of onset and duration of the trauma (van der Kolk et al., 1992). Even so, when van der Kolk (2005) proposed a DSM diagnosis of developmental trauma, it was not accepted. As a society, we seem to need to see symptoms as characteristic of the individual, rather than of their relational experience. The persistence of this in the face of the research evidence suggests something sacred may be at stake.

When a caregiver is the perpetrator of harm, if the source of the badness is questioned at all, the question becomes, am I the bad one or is s/he? The boy I mentioned in the introduction who murdered his teacher said, 'It was her or me'. The neurobiology of the internal working model (Bowlby, 1980; Siegel, 1999) implies that the distinction between his teacher and his mother may be blurred. The teacher may well have represented the primary woman in his life, to whom he could not direct his hostility. The meaning of his act is not available in the context of the present moment, but in the context of his relational history. To the outside eye it looks like madness, but in his template for relating, it might well be about nothing less than his own survival, in a fight or flight response that has not the benefit of mediation by the prefrontal cortex, which would need to be relationally wired in. This murder, appalling and tragic for the victim and her family, is itself likely to be a symptom of the tragedy of relational trauma.

In this and in less extreme cases, disturbed and disturbing behaviour is a symptom in search of a mind to recognize its import. My point here is that the intention and response of the (m)other person is crucial; an act is not alone defined by the intention of the person displaying the symptom. Language or behaviour becomes communication not only through the intention to be understood, but also through the intention and capacity to understand and respond.

In order to illustrate this process, I would like to offer three scenarios from meaning-making partnerships, one from ordinary domestic life, and two from clinical situations. The first little vignette exemplifies laying the groundwork for a relational story that can acknowledge, wonder about and respond to the child's impulses. The second account shows what happens when an overwhelmed and preoccupied mother cannot notice the child's impulse and insists on an imposed meaning or none at all. In the third scenario, I will trace the development of a rift between experience and story so wide as to induce psychosis.

First, the situation that Winnicott called 'good enough', in which a mother has sufficient internal and external resources to be able to keep an open mind about what might be going on for her baby. Winnicott's phrase has been much quoted in children's services, sometimes in a spirit of 'that'll do', which seems to have been quite the reverse of the original meaning, in which the bar is set quite high. His point is that the 'ordinary devoted mother' (Winnicott, 1957) on the whole met this exacting standard with surprising virtuosity, provided she was properly supported. I will give a brief example now of the everyday responsive connection between a well-supported mother and her baby that brings to both the delight that, along with the capacity to express anger, sadness, and the full orchestral range of feelings, lays the foundation for good mental health.

Evie was nine weeks old. She was smiling and lively as her mother, Rebecca, played with her after changing her nappy, kneeling on the floor in front of her. Rebecca leant towards her, widening her eyes and opening her mouth in a gentle emotional crescendo, holding Evie's absorbed gaze. She brightened her face in a moment of discovery, and said in a gentle, singsong voice: 'There you are!' Evie beamed and wriggled her whole body with delight. Her mouth opened wide, and Rebecca's did too, in playful imitation. Evie turned her gaze away to gather herself for a moment, and Rebecca gradually softened her face and body, sitting back and dropping the emotional tone a bit. Evie turned to catch her mother's eyes again and the whole sequence was replayed. This time, once Evie turned away her gaze seemed to be held by something to the side of her. Rebecca asked, 'What have you seen?' She looked the same way, and saw light reflected on the wall. 'Is that lovely, are you looking at the light?' she asked, with a musical intonation. Evie turned back to face her and cooed, and Rebecca cooed back in a gentle, joyful kind of way, 'What are you telling me? Was that lovely? Was it?' There was a beautiful to and fro for a little while, and Evie's face was beatific, but then she became restless, her mouth turned down, her eyes closed and her face became a picture of misery. Rebecca turned her own mouth down a little, and said, 'Oh dear'. Evie began to cry, writhing her body & clutching her hands into fists above her head. Her mother's face showed concern, and she said sympathetically, 'Ah, what's the matter, baby girl – is your tummy hurting?' She picked her up and put her against her shoulder, rubbing her back. Evie quietened, and brought her fist towards her mouth. She burped, and a dribble of milk came out of her mouth. Rebecca soothed her, 'Ah, there we are, little one, that's what it was!' Evie stayed snug against her mother's body, her head heavy on her shoulder. After rocking to and fro for a little while, Rebecca turned her head to look at her and said gently, 'Are you tired now?' She bent over the cot to lay her down, but this prompted a sad face and more crying. 'Don't you want to go down, no?' her mother asked, shaking her head as if on Evie's behalf as she looked at her. She lifted her back close against her own body. 'You need a cuddle, don't you?' She wrapped her arms around her and rocked gently to and fro.

This baby was a lucky baby, whose mother was supported and could see her daughter, reflect her feelings and respond to her needs, without present difficulties or her own care experiences preoccupying her mind too much. This level of moment-to-moment availability is extremely demanding though, and if nobody was looking after Rebecca, the work would soon become overwhelming.

I have written elsewhere (Sutton, 2014) about how the relationship with the maternal mind frames and thus limits experience that might otherwise be overwhelming. Rebecca's face reflected a little sadness when Evie cried, but not too much. Her daughter's crying was not impossible for her to bear; unlike, for example, a mother whose own cries have not been heard (Daws, 1989:174). When the maternal mind is itself overwhelmed, whether for this reason or another, the mutual meaning-making process is disturbed. The mother's mind is preoccupied with managing her own disturbing experience; her child has no way of understanding what happens and can feel the terror of being lost in meaningless space. In order to avoid this terror and establish some kind of meaning, the pair can between them unconsciously attribute the disturbance to the child.

In our second scenario, something like this seemed to be happening for a three-year-old girl whom I will call Aisha. She was referred to a child mental health clinic for head-banging and rages. Her language was rather delayed; she expressed herself chiefly through her body and was often dysregulated and distressed. Her birth had been difficult and protracted, painful and frightening for all concerned. She was born, too, into a time of grieving, days after a family bereavement. The following vignette describes the scene in the room when her mother, Anita, brought her to the clinic and began to tell the tale.

Aisha screamed in an urgent way, ran to the door and tried to get out of the room. She wrestled with the door handle, trying and failing to escape. She conveyed a feeling that the world had gone out of control and she was at terrible risk, even though her mother was present. There was a sense that far from experiencing the relief and regulation of protection in her mother's presence, Aisha was desperately trying to get out before the emotional flood level rose and engulfed her. Anita looked at the therapist in a long-suffering way that seemed to call for a witness to her exhausted compliance. She said wearily, 'Here we go, another meltdown', which evoked the idea of a nuclear reactor, utterly beyond human influence and potentially devastating for all life.

Aisha spotted a toy ambulance, gave up on the door and grabbed it, making alarming siren noises as she struggled to get the doors open and put people in it. She tried especially hard to force a figure into the driving seat. She showed the therapist the empty driving seat and said, 'No one in there!' She made the ambulance rattle around the table and then teeter on the edge, seeming to show just how close catastrophe was felt to be. She looked at the therapist urgently, conveying a sense that rescue is desperately needed, but the ambulance driver is missing and the means of rescue itself teeters or falls.

As Anita engaged the therapist with her traumatic life story and the very real difficulties she was managing in her present circumstances, there seemed to be a 'her or me' choice to be made. The therapist felt her attention pulled between the two of them, as though only one of the pair could swim into mind and the other would sink, or even perhaps be pushed under.

I will think more about the unspeakability of maternal ambivalence in the next chapter, 'It's not you, it's me: Oedipus was framed'. Here though, I would like to note that the all-pervading despair flooding through Anita at times had a detrimental impact on her capacity to bring feelings to mind, her own or Aisha's, to reflect upon them and thus stay on an even keel. Unlike Rebecca in the previous vignette, Anita was not in a position to make herself available as a partner in the dance of connection. She was preoccupied with her own powerful emotions, and lacked a responsive partner of her own to help find meaning and regulate them. She seemed to need to insist on the meaninglessness that was her experience. This overwhelmed and overwhelming maternal state of mind seems to have meant Aisha expressed powerful emotions, not just her own, through her body. I think there was a catastrophe to be feared, but it had already happened; it was a catastrophe her mother had already experienced. That is to say, I think perhaps some of Aisha's difficulties were to be understood in the context of Anita's post-traumatic stress symptoms, arising from significant adversity without much relational buffering in her life history and triggered by the trauma of Aisha's painful birth during a time of complicated grief. Nobody was there to 'mind' Anita, and Anita was unable to 'mind' Aisha.

Out of this relational context, Aisha's episodes of dysregulation seemed unpredictable and meaningless. Anita lived in fear of her 'meltdowns' and understood them as inflicted upon her in a randomly frightening way. Thus in her mother's response to her, Aisha sometimes found a mind overwhelmed by actual and potential past and present difficulties, entangled with her feelings and continually on the verge of a catastrophe which had already happened. The feeling of this is then woven into the pattern of what happens between the two of them, and becomes foundational for Aisha's sense of herself in relation to the world. Seeing Aisha's ensuing dysregulation as an individual symptom obscures the relational dynamics, the forceful disruption that was happening between them. Without intervention that supports not only Aisha but also her mother, these patterns can shape her internal world, and the emotional world she lives in, for the rest of her life.

The third vignette I will turn to now shows how wide the rift between experience and the narrative account can be. It derives from a clinical situation in which the response of the meaning-making partner is to deny and distort in order to protect the equilibrium of a family system. Adam's anorexic symptoms at thirteen years old were as lodged in the body as Aisha's and, as I will try to show, just as much to be seen in the context of his parents' states of mind and a tangle of family identifications. Unlike Aisha, though, Adam seemed not to be looking to escape, but tightening the locks.

His mother described him as very much like his father and grandfather, both of whom had suffered from severe depression. Before he was four, his parents separated and his father committed suicide. In what follows, I hope to illuminate the striking contrast between the cheerful lightness of being with him and his mother together, and the tragic weight of his life history, expressed in the dark, heavy feeling of being with him on his own, an emotional quality that was disavowed in their relationship.

During the initial family meeting, Adam said little, peeping out from behind a thick curtain of hair, and letting his mother do the talking for him. 'He was a wonderful baby', she said with delighted pride. There was a youthful air about her, and the pair seemed like close siblings without a care in the world as they sat together on the sofa, smiling shyly. 'He takes after his dad', his mother confided; and it was a struggle to remember that his father had committed suicide. Her tone conveyed a total disavowal of pain; it was almost encouraging, as if she was saying he might follow his father into some line of work.

Shortly afterwards, in an individual session:

After a long, heavy silence, Adam drew a black scribbly cloud and put a firm grid of lines across it. He crumpled the page up and wanted to bin it, and then started to pace up and down the room on a fixed line. The pacing continued. He seemed to be walking a narrow line over a dark cloud of feelings that would be terrifying to fall into. There was a wary, watchful quality. He conveyed a sense of a steely 'border guard' part of him on patrol, to prevent things coming out, and stop dreadful things coming in. Occasional glances from behind his heavy fringe let his therapist see that behind this 'border patrol' part of him, another, more vulnerable part might be hiding. He eventually volunteered that he'd like to get back to the days when he was so thin he was in danger of having a heart attack.

He became excited by this idea, and talked in an animated way about wanting to be in a near death situation.

The extremity of what he conveyed was shockingly at odds with the brittle, shiny atmosphere of being with Adam and his mother together, when they were almost defiantly smiley, as if to forestall or reject enquiry or concern. The cheeriness may well have been the story the relationship could bear, but it does not fit with the urgency of a near death situation. The stance of 'this is not happening' inevitably meant a rupture in the relationship with other people's experience of reality – the hallmark of psychosis. It did convey, though, an essential truth about the relationship with reality established in the formative meaning-making partnership with his mother.

In the clinical world, people talk of 'presenting symptoms', and I think it is clinically useful to think about what (and who) it might be that the symptom makes present. I wonder if Adam's anorexia was his way of embodying a link with a suicidal father. Perhaps it was a way of trying to keep him present, rather than lose him, even though or perhaps because he already had.

There was a sense of unspeakable feelings, and little faith that they could be conveyed to anyone, other than by the symptom of not eating. The idea that he could find a responsive partner with whom to build his capacity for digesting emotional experience felt as much threat as opportunity for him. It would risk the fragile status quo he was managing through the symptom. In his relational experience, there was nowhere for his terror to go, and so he protected the relationship with his (m)other by keeping it at bay.

I will come back to the importance of preserving, even protecting, the symptom in the chapter, 'Getting your own back: revisiting resistance', but it is worth noting that the dilemma relates to the question of responsibility I mentioned in the introduction. I am emphasizing the response in responsibility here. Given the kind of care constellation we saw in the first vignette, the mother's responsive sensibility defines the relationship, seeks and establishes meaning, receives, regulates and translates the qualities of emotional experience the baby conveys. As Fairbairn (1952) suggests, it may be this responsive sensibility that establishes a sense of goodness, and its lack a sense of badness. Without a good enough care constellation, or when a traumatic event breaks through it, the experience gets lodged in the body, as it did for Aisha and for Adam, until someone can finally bear to get the message.

Body language and trauma

Freud's experience treating medically unexplained symptoms led him to notice how symptoms act as the body's symbols:

> We might perhaps suppose that the patient had formed an association between her painful mental impressions and the bodily pains which she happened to be experiencing at the same time, and that now, in her life of memories, she was using her physical feelings as a symbol of her mental ones.
>
> (Breuer & Freud, 1895:144)

His link between bodily pains and painful mental impressions prefigures Hebb's (1949) law by which neurons that fire together, wire together, creating neural networks of associated impressions, ideas, and feelings. Freud's definition of trauma is that which pierces the protective shield of the mental apparatus; there is no mental schema, no representation. He suggests that patients suffering from trauma as Adam was 'are more concerned with not thinking of it' (Freud, 1924:282). However, despite conscious or unconscious attempts to withdraw from a shocking reality in the service of maintaining some kind of social functioning, in psychoses and in post-traumatic stress disorder (PTSD), bad feelings associated with the trauma break through the disavowal.

Neurobiologically, what happens is that the hippocampus, part of the limbic system dealing with emotion and involved with the assigning of time and place signatures to body memory, is flooded by cortisol in response to stress. Its function is thereby disrupted, or even damaged. In this way, the protective stress response weakens the ability of the memory system to keep a diary, as it were, to form explicit locatable memories. In PTSD then, the amygdala triggers an immediate response to bad feelings, without the person concerned being aware of their origin, because the hippocampus was flooded by cortisol and could not form a conscious explicit memory.

Bucci (2011) suggests that dissociations occur in response to events that are extremely painful, experienced as threats to life or to the organization of the self. If the caregiver is the source of the traumatic experience, avoidant dissociation is inevitable. In a disorganized attachment where the caregiver is frightened or frightening, the child needs to avoid knowing the source of the extreme pain in order to go on with life, because of physical and emotional dependence on the caregiver.

Once this dissociation is wired in, it becomes the symptom that prevents change. We have seen how the brain functions as an anticipation machine (Siegel, 1999), and it is safer in the context of this dangerous relational past to assume that this is what we will meet in the future. When this kind of implicit knowledge is survival-related, it is prioritized.

It has become crystal clear, then, that we cannot detach the symptom from the implicit relational experience. Freud's is a one-person psychology, and later thinkers, perhaps Bion and Winnicott particularly in the psychoanalytic tradition, develop his theory to include the mind of the (m)other as formative. Freud's concept of repression excludes what is unacceptable to part of the self, but Bion's and Winnicott's theories go further in looking at the derivation of such a prohibition. If there is no such thing as a baby (Winnicott, 1960), developmentally speaking, only a mother-baby dyad, we have the roots not just of internalized objects (Klein, 1959) but of relationships too (Fairbairn, 1952) and qualities of experience (Bion, 1962), which Stern (1998) has called 'ways-of-being-with'. Another way of seeing repression is that unacceptable aspects of experience go unrepresented in that primary relationship. The prohibitive relationship is then internalized, so that internal awareness is not possible, either, despite the efforts of the nervous system to express the nature of the felt experience. Something about the experience is incompatible with the received representation of the (m)other, and thus perhaps the relationship with her. At a more extreme point on the continuum, psychosis might be the result of an experience incompatible with any coherent and integrated representation of the qualities of the relationship.

Symptoms of psychosis overlap with those of a post-traumatic state of mind. In fact the British Psychological Society's (2014) *Understanding Psychosis* states:

> Indeed there is no way of clearly separating 'psychotic' experiences … from problems resulting from trauma which might attract diagnoses such as 'post-traumatic stress' or 'personality disorder'.

Perhaps at the root of the symptoms we are considering here is the terrifying feeling that primitive fears cannot be made sense of, that they belong to no relational context that might give them meaning –

Bion's nameless dread (1962:116), Winnicott's fear of falling forever (1974:103).

Therapeutically, holding someone responsible for the fear, that is, having someone to respond to it, to feel its power while also taking the associated hatred; representing the primary object in the terms of the transference, and taking compassionate responsibility for the failures of holding, seems to offer a way forward. The proviso is that careful attention is paid to what the patient can bear, 'a piecemeal step at a time' (Alvarez, 2012:20). This paves the way for new ways of being, involving emergent properties of the nervous system and the mind, making use of multiple representations of lived experience. Research has shown that internal representations develop through successive developmental states (Blatt et al., 1990), so that change can begin to happen internally, through implicit experience. The evidence is that we need another mind to help us move from re-presenting extreme states of mind, re-enacting them in the present, towards symbolic representation at one remove from the experience, so that we can find a relation to it, rather than be trapped in a repetition of the past in the present. Clinical experience with children who have suffered trauma suggests that alongside the new ways of being in the new relationship, there does need to be some representation of the old order (Sutton, 2014), otherwise new experiences can feel like the old re-presented with a mask, because of their inherent danger to a child whose psychobiological system is adapted to danger. The way in which therapeutic attention is paid to the tiniest shifts in this nuanced process is the subject of much of the work of Alvarez (2012), and will be addressed in the final chapter. Here though, I would like to mention that it seems to be about attending to the how of experience, rather than the what, to the musical qualities of the present connection at least as much as its content.

Pally's work on memory supports this view. In writing about the reconstructive properties of memory processing, she describes how what is later remembered is constructed in the here and now, together with all the sensory and emotional impressions of the present moment, and is not an exact replica of what happened in the past. 'All the neural elements involved in the processing of events serve as new information to be stored as additional memory traces of the event' (Pally, 1997:1229). These new neural elements include the qualities of the present relationship, including a representation of the search for meaning, Bion's (1962) getting to know.

When a parent, or later perhaps a therapist, is able to make themselves available for the demanding work of getting to know what it feels like, through emotional resonance and then reflection upon the qualities of that experience, there can be developmental change. The question of what happens when nobody wants to know, or nobody can bear to know, is worth exploring. When this happens, it may be that the symptom a child expresses serves a function for the whole family system. I will turn now to consider this possibility.

The symptom as a container for parental distress and vulnerability

Bion's idea of containment implies a process; not so much a place to put things as a way of getting to know what they feel like. His concept involves regulation and meaning-seeking in the service of development. The symptom can be used for two of these three purposes, if maintaining the status quo rather than development is the aim, precluding change and development.

We have seen that research from the disciplines of neuroscience and child development points to the importance of the maternal function in regulating feelings and creating meaning. Schore (2003) describes what happens in the infant brain when this process does not happen. He connects impairments of the early development of the right brain's stress coping systems with damaged infant mental health. For example, in the symptoms for which Aisha was referred, I think we were seeing her underdeveloped stress coping system overloaded.

The significance of this for her developing mind is hard to overestimate. Self-and-other awareness develops in infancy (Trevarthen & Aitken, 2001). An infant's biologically grounded self-regulation and sense of meaning are connected, and sustained through actively engaging with sympathetic people around them. There are thus significant negative implications for self-regulation, for mutual creation of meaning, and for attuned self- awareness when the active engagement of a sympathetic person is simply not available. Thus when a good enough care constellation is missing because of adverse circumstances, a child's development can go awry, as we saw with Aisha and Adam.

The trajectory is exponential; dysregulation can eventually evoke despair, and as Klein's work (1975) has shown, we do need someone to represent the badness. We would rather be subject to a world dominated by a bad figure than to meaningless chaos – we could not survive in a world in which connection itself is bad, so children claim the badness in the clinically familiar way of seeing themselves as bad. This can set up a vicious circle, whereby once a child is seen to embody badness, they have no way of metabolizing the bad feeling other than by the symptom, which confirms them as the source of badness in their own and their parents' eyes. If we consider the age-old question of who profits from the arrangement, this dynamic begins to look convenient. Aisha, for example, has been seen by her mother as subject to unpredictable rages that cannot be explained; and also at times as the source of meaningless attack. To put it another way, what her mother found overwhelming, even persecutory, was seen to be her. Anita needed somewhere to locate unprocessed fears, and Aisha's underdeveloped coping system made her an obvious though unconscious choice. Anita could locate the disturbance, a bad feeling which readily represents a kind of generalized badness, in Aisha.

Williams (1997) describes a 'no-entry' system of defences, in response to projections aimed at the child by the parent and felt to be persecutory. Adam seems to have constructed a 'keep out' defence, and patrolled it vigorously, but Aisha does not seem to have been able to erect any such barrier. She had very little protection from the emotional overload on her nervous system and resorted not so much to a state of mind as a state of body, thrashing around, out of her own and her mother's control. To some extent, this could be translated into a state of mind by the therapeutic process. But that meant she had to find a new place in her mother's mind, and then what would she do with the disturbance? This has been a dilemma in the practice of child psychotherapy as cuts have decimated services and limited work with parents. Working individually with children, therapists risk leaving children in a relation to their parents that destroys the old order, releasing a disturbance that the family system cannot bear.

Both Aisha and Adam in their different ways were in a situation Waddell describes where

> not only does [the child] not have a mind into which he can project his distress, but [his] distress becomes augmented both by the discovery that this is so and by the fact that the weight of his own feelings is now being added to. For the presence which should be relieving him of distress is now actively increasing it.
> (2002:48)

This process has been described as incorporation of an invasive object (Williams, 2010), in which the relationship with an overwhelmed and overwhelming object creates an experience of being flooded. The idea is that this pattern of incorporation happens when a mother has great difficulty resonating with the infant's experience, and instead dominates with her own, especially when the balancing support of other minds is compromised or absent. He calls attention to the internalization of this quality of domination. If something similar was happening for Aisha, it may be no surprise that during the last phase of therapy, she brought with her monster trucks that rode roughshod over everything.

Unlike Evie's mother, it seemed to be very hard sometimes for Aisha's and Adam's mothers to think of their child as having a mind of their own, and as behaving in response to the people around them. Instead, when Aisha's mother was overwhelmed, and Adam's mother was faced with the unthinkable, they each tended to attribute their own meaning or the lack of it to their child. Child development research suggests that their children will have internalized the qualities of this relationship. The situation is then exponentially reinforced, for good or ill. Siegel explains how the process works:

> The ways in which neural circuits anticipate experience may help us understand how the mind develops through a recursive set of interactions. As representational processes anticipate experience, they also seek particular forms of interactions to match their expectations. In this way, the "bias" of a system leads it to perceive, process, and act in a particular manner. The outcome of this bias is to reinforce the very features creating the system's bias.
>
> (1999:305)

A child's developing brain will wire in, anticipate and then seek the particular relational experience he or she experiences, so that neural pathways are reinforced. Evie will tend to evoke concerned responsive relationships; Aisha and Adam, until another mind becomes available – for example in the process of psychotherapy – will tend to evoke the qualities of their very different early relational experience. For each child, their mother's availability as a partner in meaning-seeking and emotional regulation is therefore formative. Perhaps the extent of the problem depends upon the extent to which the mother is already occupied, haunted by the ghosts in her nursery (Fraiberg et al., 1975), dominated by the anticipation machine of her mind and thus unable to see her child.

We are profoundly social, profoundly meaning-making creatures. The two are inter-linked. We seek meaning through connection with others that creates the story of who we are, of who we need to be in our own particular social setting to find our place and belong. When traumatic early experience has failed to produce a coherent story, and/or produced a story in which we are the source of badness, this provokes conflict with the fact of our own existence. A new relational story needs to be created that understands disturbance as happening in relationship. In this way a new representation of badness is possible, as a dynamic quality rather than a personal attribute. Unless and until someone gets it, the symptom in search of meaning continues to present itself.

References

Alvarez, A. (2012). *The Thinking Heart: Three Levels of Psychoanalytic Therapy with Disturbed Children*. London: Routledge.

Beebe, B. & Lachmann, F. (2002). *Infant Research and Adult Treatment: Co-constructing Interactions*. London: Analytic.

Bion, W. R. (1962). *Learning from Experience*. London: Heinemann.

Blatt, S. J., Quinlan, D. M., & Chevron, E. (1990). Empirical investigations of a psychoanalytic theory of depression. In J. Masling (Ed.), *Empirical Studies of Psychoanalytic Theories*, Vol. 3:89–147. New Jersey: Analytic.

Bowlby, J. (1969). *Attachment and Loss*, Vol. 1. New York: Basic.

Bowlby, J. (1980). *Attachment and Loss*, Vol. 3. New York: Basic.

Braten, S. (1992). The virtual other in infants' minds and social feelings. In A. H. Wold (Ed.), *The Dialogical Alternative*:77–97. Oslo: Scandinavian University.

Breuer, J. & Freud, S. (1895). Studies in hysteria. In J. Strachey (Ed.), *The Standard Edition of the Complete Psychological Works of Sigmund Freud*, Vol. 2:1–335. London: Hogarth.

British Psychological Society. (2014). *Understanding Psychosis*. Retrieved from www1.bps.org.uk/system/files/user-files/Division%20of%20Clinical%20Psychology/public/CAT-1657.pdf.

Bucci, W. (2011). The role of subjectivity and intersubjectivity in the reconstruction of dissociated schemas: Converging perspectives from psychoanalysis, cognitive science and affective neuroscience. *Psychoanalytic Psychology*, 28(2):247–266.

Damasio, A. (1999). *The Feeling of What Happens: Body and Mind in the Making of Consciousness*. Florida: Harcourt.

Daws, D. (1989). *Through the Night: Helping Parents and Sleepless Infants*. London: Free Association.

Fairbairn, W. R. D. (1952). *Psychoanalytic Studies of the Personality*. London: Routledge.

Fraiberg, S., Adelson, E., & Shapiro, V. (1975). Ghosts in the nursery: A psychoanalytic approach to the problems of impaired infant-mother relationships. *Journal of the American Academy of Child & Adolescent Psychiatry*, 14(3):387–421.

Freud, S. (1897). Abstracts of the scientific works of Dr. Sigmund Freud, 1877–1897. In J. Strachey (Ed.), *The Standard Edition of the Complete Psychological Works of Sigmund Freud*, Vol. 3:227–256. London: Hogarth.

Freud, S. (1924). Neurosis and psychosis. In J. Strachey (Ed. & Trans.), *The Standard Edition of the Complete Psychological Works of Sigmund Freud*, Vol. 19:149–153. London: Hogarth.

Goldsmith, J. & Cowen, H. (2011). The inheritance of loss. *Journal of Child Psychotherapy*, 37(2):179–193.

Hebb, D. O. (1949). *The Organization of Behavior*. New York: Wiley.

Kisilevsky, B. S., Hains, S. M., Brown, C. A., Lee, C. T., Cowperthwaite, B., Stutzman, S. S., Swansburg, M. L., Lee, K., Xie, X., Huang, H., Ye, H. H., Zhang, K., & Wang, Z. (2009). Fetal sensitivity to properties of maternal speech and language. *Infant Behavioral Development*, 32(1):59–71.

Klein, M. (1946). Notes on some schizoid mechanisms. In B. Joseph, E. O'Shaughnessy, & H. Segal (Eds.), *Envy and Gratitude & Other Works, 1946–1963*:1–24. London: Hogarth, 1975.

Klein, M. (1959). Our adult world and its roots in infancy. In B. Joseph, E. O'Shaughnessy, & H. Segal (Eds.), *Envy and Gratitude & Other Works, 1946–1963*:247–263. London: Hogarth, 1975.

McDougall, J. (1989). *Theatres of the Body: A Psychoanalytical Approach to Psychosomatic Illness*. London: Free Association.

Pally, R. (1997). Memory: Brain systems that link past, present and future. *International Journal of Psychoanalysis*, 78(6):1223–1234.

Schore, A. N. (2003). *Affect Dysregulation and Disorders of the Self*. New York: Norton.

Schutz, L. E. (2005). Broad-perspective perceptual disorder of the right hemisphere. *Neuropsychology Review*, 15:11–27.

Siegel, D. J. (1999). *The Developing Mind: Toward a Neurobiology of Interpersonal Experience*. New York: Guilford.

Steiner, J. (1985). Turning a blind eye: The cover up for Oedipus. *International Review of Psychoanalysis*, 12:161–172.

Steiner, J. (1993). *Psychic Retreats: Pathological Organisations in Psychotic, Neurotic and Borderline Patients*. London: Routledge.

Stern, D. (1998). The process of therapeutic change involving implicit knowledge: Some implications of developmental observations for adult psychotherapy. *Infant Mental Health Journal*, 19:300–308.

Suomi, S. J. (1984). The development of affect in Rhesus monkeys. In N. Fox & R. Davidson (Eds.), *The Psychology of Affective Development*:119–159. Hillsdale, NJ: Lawrence Erlbaum.

Sutton, S. (2014). *Being Taken In: The Framing Relationship*. London: Karnac.
Trevarthen, C. (2005). First things first: Infants make good use of the sympathetic rhythm of imitation, without reason or language. *Journal of Child Psychotherapy*, 31(1):91–113.
Trevarthen, C. & Aitken, K. J. (2001). Infant intersubjectivity: Research, theory, and clinical applications. *Journal of Child Psychology & Psychiatry*, 42:3–48.
van der Kolk, B. A. (2005). Developmental trauma disorder: Towards a rational diagnosis for children with complex trauma histories. *Psychiatric Annals*, 25(5):401–408.
van der Kolk, B. A. & Ducey, C. P. (1989). The psychological processing of traumatic experience: Rorschach patterns in PTSD. *Journal of Traumatic Stress*, 2:259–274.
van der Kolk, B. A., Roth, S., & Pelcovitz, D. (1992). *Field Trials for DSM IV, Post Traumatic Stress Disorder II: Disorders of Extreme Stress*. Washington, DC: American Psychiatric Association.
Waddell, M. (2002). *Inside Lives: Psychoanalysis and the Growth of the Personality*. London: Tavistock.
Williams, G. (1997). *Internal Landscapes and Foreign Bodies: Eating Disorders and Other Pathologies*. London: Duckworth.
Williams, P. (2010). The incorporation of an invasive object. In J. van Buren & S. Alhanati (Eds.), *Primitive Mental States: A Psychoanalytic Exploration of the Origins of Meaning*:47–63. New York: Routledge.
Winnicott, D. (1960). The theory of the parent-infant relationship. In D. Winnicott (Ed.), *The Maturational Processes and the Facilitating Environment*:37–55. New York: International Universities.
Winnicott, D. W. (1957). The ordinary devoted mother and her baby. In D. Winnicott (Ed.), *The Child and the Family*. London: Tavistock. (Original work published 1949)
Winnicott, D. W. (1974). Fear of Breakdown. *International Review of Psychoanalysis*, 1:103–107.
Zalidis, S. (2009). Tears: Emotional or somatic? *Psychoanalytic Psychotherapy*, 23(4):321–329.

Chapter 3

It's not you, it's me

Oedipus was framed

The myth of the individual mind is exploded by the last three decades of brain research, which shows the profoundly formative influence of the baby's relationship with the parents, inevitably infused with the ghosts of their unremembered pasts. In this chapter, I will revisit that cornerstone of psychoanalytic thinking, the Oedipus complex, in the light of the relational nature of mind and identity brought into focus by modern neuroscience. The contemporary psychoanalytic thinker Britton (1989) has shown how this triangular relationship opens ground for becoming aware of ourselves from other perspectives, for witnessing as well as experiencing. Thus the narrative of our lives is created. What can be included in this narrative, as I have suggested earlier, influences the scope of what can be included in our sense of ourselves, and so lays the groundwork for our mental health. When we feel emotions and impulses that are outside the received and receivable narrative, there is conflict. The strength and depth of the conflict depends on the force of the emotional impact of our circumstances, when nobody is prepared to bear witness.

The first person to bear witness to the child's experience is typically the parent. The nature and impact of the parental perception of the child's experience is perhaps understudied outside the field of parent infant mental health. From that field, Jones writes of how, during the process of parent-infant psychotherapy, 'as the projected aspects of the parent are reclaimed, the baby becomes freer to be noticed as a separate being with thoughts and feelings of its own' (2006:109). Although much important work has been done on the intergenerational transmission of trauma, especially since the Holocaust, in psychiatry and indeed in everyday life we often seem to stop short of seeing what the child becomes for the parent, given that parent's early world.

Reframing mental health symptoms as expressions of that which is known but cannot be thought about in the early world offers a way of redressing that imbalance. I will consider here parental projection, of which the Oedipus complex is an interesting example, focusing as it does on the (unwitting) death-dealing and consequent marriage of the son, and not on the original hostility of the father, whose fear of his son and attempt to kill him set in train the whole sorry business.

We will look at the formative constellation of relationships establishing our sense of identity, and the powerful role of parental projections in this process. We will consider the dependency of children upon their parents, a power balance towards which we have on the whole in the mental health world turned a blind eye. In talking about identity, we need a way of talking about the edit, the account we are given which we then give of ourselves. This way of talking needs to be situated between the worlds of art and of science, to acknowledge the interplay between the physiological and the imaginative. In this way, the symptom can be seen as the body's metaphor; an experienced truth seeking expression, that has been deleted from the received version of the story.

In thinking about parental projection in the construction of identity, we will look first at some of the powerfully conflicting feelings in pregnancy and postnatal experience, which for some parents can feel polarized in the extreme: it's the baby or me. This can feel unspeakable, and no wonder: we seem to require of mothers that they devote themselves selflessly to their children. We cannot stomach maternal ambivalence and seem to need the account of motherhood to be one of self-sacrifice. Perhaps in that account, as a body we express a longing for our own mother's undivided attention, and cannot tolerate another narrative. Perhaps, too, each mother struggles to say goodbye to her own unmet needs, and pays lip service to an ideal of motherhood she still longs for.

In the context of the idealization of motherhood, there is the question of what happens to a mother's outrage at being sidelined in her own body? After all, evolution prioritizes the developmental needs of the fetus over the mother. What outlet does she have for anger that from now on, to a greater or lesser extent, her life is an adjunct to someone else's, whose needs she must serve on pain of their death? She has, in effect, become a part in someone else's story, rather than the main event. Klein's ideas offer an available location for the inexpressible rage, conveniently near at hand – the baby itself. She begins by acknowledging that the idea of a young baby trying to destroy its mother by every means at its disposal 'with its teeth, nails, and excreta and with the whole of its body transformed in phantasy into all kinds of dangerous weapons – presents a horrifying, not to say an unbelievable picture to our minds' (1932:130). She asserts, however, 'that the abundance, force and multiplicity of the cruel phantasies which accompany these cravings are displayed before our eyes in early analyses so clearly and forcefully that they leave no room for doubt' (ibid).

The Kleinian baby then is seen to have arrived in the world with 'sadistic trends' (Klein, 1932:130) for which it fears retaliation. Furthermore, the baby is seen as desiring to burrow into the mother's body and steal all the good things inside her that she withholds for her own pleasure. Building on this phantasy attack and theft in quite a sophisticated way for a relatively unformed mind, without the agenda of the left brain, which is at this stage undeveloped, having projected these impulses out onto the mother and then taken in a version of the mother with these attributes, 'the child comes to imagine a Terrible Mother figure that desires to rip open, suck dry and devour him' (Klein, 1932:130). And so in this convoluted way, it becomes possible for the idea of the Terrible Mother to be attributed to hateful impulses within the child. We have to ask ourselves whether it is more convincing that the mother or the baby feels this degree of hatred, given the strictures imposed on the mother by the baby's vulnerable dependency, and the taboo on maternal outrage.

So mothers seem to be seen on the whole as more hated than hating in the Kleinian account. We will turn now to examine the Freudian idea of the Oedipal setup, which sees sons wishing to destroy their fathers, and turns a blind eye to fathers' fear of being usurped.

Whose death wish is it anyway?

In the myth of Oedipus, a little baby boy is feared by his father the king and left tethered out on a mountainside to die. He is rescued and survives, and the next time the two men meet, his father tries to run him over, and is killed himself. Answering a riddle to release the city of his birth from thrall then sets the young man up to marry the widowed queen, his mother.

Every step of the way, hobbled by his swollen feet, the boy is doing his best to survive, struggling to make sense of his own existence despite smokescreen machinations and direct hostility from a higher power: his parents. And yet, he is represented as the archetype of desire for one parent and hostility towards the other. Surely there is some mistake here?

It seems to me that Oedipus was set up. He is caught in this life and death struggle, but he is not the protagonist. Like every baby, he is asking the question, what do I have to do to belong around here, to get protection and survive? If there is a parallel story from the point of view of the baby, would it not need to take into account the initial attempt on his life by his parents? He is feared and rejected, abandoned, and left to die.

Freud takes up the story in his account of Little Hans: 'Hans really was a little Oedipus who wanted his father out of the way. To get rid of him, so that he might be alone with his beautiful mother and sleep with her' (1909:111). He further suggests that Hans's wish for intimacy with his mother led the boy to wish his father would permanently be away – that he should be dead. Yet nowhere in the myth of Oedipus is it suggested that Oedipus wants his father to die; rather the father Laius fears his son and explicitly wants him dead. Why turn it around? Freud's idea is that the death wish aimed at the father is normal for all little boys. It is to be resolved through fear of castration by the father and consequent turning away from mother towards another love. His theory is that if the complex is not resolved in this way, it can lie at the root of all kinds of symptoms and phobias (Freud, 1909:115). The parents' role is disavowed. I will come back to consider why this might be so, but will first look at evidence from another field of enquiry.

Turning from psychoanalysis to the different but related sphere of infant mental health, the prevalence of maternal perinatal depression points to a link between the birth of a child and extremely difficult emotional experience. Between ten and twenty percent of women develop a mental illness during pregnancy or within the first year (Bauer et al., 2014). Examples include antenatal and postnatal depression, obsessive compulsive disorders, post-traumatic stress disorder, and severe postpartum psychosis. Strikingly, suicide is a leading cause of death during pregnancy and within a year of giving birth. Almost half of all perinatal depression and anxiety goes undetected. These unsettling figures are not part of the myth of motherhood. Again, it seems, something is disavowed.

Anyone who ever had a child or was a child knows that the profound and life-altering experience of parenthood is not only unalloyed joy. It can evoke overwhelming love, compassion, joy and fulfilment, and also anger, hurt, sorrow, and all the orchestral range of emotion stirred by closeness and interdependence. Children do not only love their parents either, and this is harder to talk about. The poet Larkin (1968/2018) admits guiltily in a letter to a friend, 'Sometimes I wonder if I'm fond of my mother at all', and describes his anger towards her as a fight for emotional freedom against the enemy, even though he wrote to her with devoted regularity for decades.

For some reason, it is easier to express negative emotions in relation to children than in relation to parents. Even Freud, who could contemplate most things, was more comfortable talking in early twentieth-century Vienna about sexuality as he saw it in children than in subjecting parents' emotional lives to the spotlight of his attention. He does not consider the relevance for understanding the story of Little Hans of the fact that Hans' mother had been his patient, that Hans' father was one of his friends, and that they were both Wednesday evening disciples, whom he had asked for material to explore (even, perhaps, confirm) a hypothesis around children's sexuality. Neither does he draw attention to Hans' mother's depression, nor to the fact that the couple split after the period described in the case. The impact of these undercurrents on Hans is not part of the enquiry, nor is his parents' possible use of him in offering the material to Freud. It may be the greatest betrayal, the oldest taboo, not what children feel towards adults, but what adults sometimes feel towards children. We know it – we cannot avoid knowing the worst of it, as more and more horrible revelations come to light about child abuse – but we cannot bear to know it. We cannot accuse our parents.

This makes evolutionary sense. There is a primitive bind of dependency that stretches long past its physical use-by date. Emotionally we are childlike in our desire to be loved by our parents. The philosopher de Kesel (2017) asks, what then do we do with our need to differentiate ourselves from them? He describes the dual need: I both need to be you, for you to recognize me and love me, and be different from you, to live my own life. This universal dilemma around the need to belong means the connection with parents is necessarily divided, incorporating love and hate, impulses towards and away.

It also means we are divided from ourselves, since identity is not the essence but the account, the story we tell, which can never be the whole picture and may need to exclude troubling aspects of experience. As Joyce (1926/1975) wrote, 'a great part of human existence is passed in a state which cannot be rendered sensible by the use of wideawake language, cutanddry grammar and goahead plot'. Like Freud, he was interested in dream life as an alternative account, not bound by the laws of imposed coherence that apply in day-to-day waking life. Which parts can we include in the more or less coherent account we give of ourselves? The imposition of coherence can depend on the reader, the listener, the receiver of the account. There is always a dissonance between accounts of ourselves, dream states acknowledged or unacknowledged. There are aspects of who we feel ourselves to be which we live with or not depending on the capacity of our (internalized, originally actual) parents to cope with alternatives. This in turn derives from their (internalized) capacity to be aware of their own conflicting possibilities without inflicting them on us.

Freud's version of the oedipal configuration suggests desire can be excluded from the received account. He does in fact exclude the desire of the parents to both be and differentiate themselves from their children, in his attribution of desire to the child. He concentrates specifically on the son, perhaps even more specifically the first born son of the marriage of a young woman to a much older man. Many mothers suffering from postnatal depression, though, might feel that hate at least as much as desire is excluded from acceptable accounts. It can seem in the mythologizing of motherhood that hate and the desire to get away cannot be part of the narrative and have to be turned in upon the self. We have seen that suicide is a leading cause of death in pregnancy or during the baby's first year. Part of the problem of identity for mothers, as for all of us, arising from the need to belong, is the need to make a coherent account which fits the moral frame of the social group we belong to. The very word account refers to a balance sheet, a weighing up of assets and liabilities; we give an account of ourselves that justifies our actions, often retrospectively.

In relation to this idea of an account, a version of events, Britton's (1989) ideas about the Oedipus complex are relevant. He considers the role of the internal triangle, representing links between child and parents, in the growth of knowledge and mental life. Much of his work examines the nature of belief, imagination, and self-awareness. He proposes that the stance of holding a belief as opposed to recognizing a fact requires the capacity to bring together subjective experience with self-awareness, so that one can see oneself believing. He sees this as requiring the presence of triangular psychic space, formed by three elements. There is an aspect of perceived reality, there is someone doing the perceiving, and there is also someone aware of them perceiving. Participants can shift between positions.

His view is that this process establishes the internalized Oedipus complex as the basis of psychic reality for each of us. In the light of this perspective, we might say that the child's relation to the parents' relationship and vice versa is crucial for establishing the ground they stand on. It seems from the development research (Hobson, 2002) that the qualities of engagement in these relationships constitute the very way we think.

Britton's (1989) focus clinically is on toleration of this constellation of relationships or the lack of it. Can we bear to witness the parental relationship, or is it felt to destroy the twoness we need and so we deny it and defend ourselves against it? He considers the clinical relevance of defences against awareness of it, including what he calls 'Oedipal illusions' (1989:85) which preclude curiosity and the process of getting to know. It would seem to be clear from the neuroscience we have looked at in earlier chapters that the capacity to take in or defend ourselves against this constellation is in direct relation to its qualities, rather than to any predisposition in the child. Is it compatible with the child's own presence in the world? Do the relationships within it feel welcoming, engaging, and curious? Or is the child sequestered by one or other or both parents in service of some missing element? Does it even require the child to identify with a view of him or herself as intolerable – it's her/him or me? Britton describes how his own thinking during sessions was experienced like a kind of parental coming together, which some of his patients felt threatened their existence. My thought is, perhaps this apprehension of a threat to life represents an experienced truth. Perhaps the parental relationship did threaten the child's existence. Perhaps this is the death wish excluded from the psychoanalytic account of childhood: not a child's towards a parent, but a parent's towards a child.

Psychoanalysis, the Oedipus complex, and power

It may be that moralizing is what we do when there is something we cannot take in. Better to blame and to get one's retaliation in first than to have to see from a different perspective, which may be felt to preclude one's own. In principle, psychoanalysis offers another perspective, providing it questions its own assumptions, acting as witness and not judge; providing morality does not come into it. We need morality to be a sorting principle, an ordering principle, but psychoanalysis is not concerned with order, rather with truth, which lives with contradictions and conflict and unsolvable problems. Who for instance is responsible in the case of the boy I mentioned right at the beginning, who stabbed his teacher? If we need to take a moral stance, who do we blame? Where does the violence stop? As a society, in our moralizing, we tend to choose those who cannot retaliate. I mentioned that the urge to attack when shame threatens to be overwhelming is protective, even though it is also destructive. Whose life is then privileged, prioritized? Who is protected, who gets destroyed? The Oedipus complex as it is widely understood insists on destroying the child, in that it projects onto the child that which the parent cannot acknowledge, making the child in the image of the parent's fears. Similarly, Baldwin (1965) argues that racism emerges from black identity as conceived in the white mind, consisting of all the monstrosity of slave-owning that white identity disavows. Social justice systems worldwide decide on badness and goodness, and on the whole tend towards blaming the victims of wider crimes of established power. More black men are incarcerated in the US, fighting the idea of themselves perpetrated by slavery and white power; more fostered children are in detention centres, punished for their lack of a loving home and the capacities that grow from it. The starving poor were transported across the world in previous centuries for stealing food when industrialists had removed their means of making a living. As the early English folk poem has it:

> The law locks up the man or woman
> Who steals the goose from off the common
> But leaves the greater villain loose
> Who steals the common from the goose.

We punish those who have suffered our attempts to annihilate them and turn a blind eye to the injustice of the power imbalance.

I think a psychic version of human sacrifice can happen for children in families, as their least powerful members. The classic idea of the Oedipus complex can be understood as a kind of oppression, the violence of projected desire. There are all kinds of qualities in their children that parents wish for: if only I had my time again, if only I was young again, if only I had your capacities, if only I had had a mother or father to love me as you have in me. I want to be you and have what you have – these feelings are at least as true of parents as they are of their children. More troublingly, struggling parents may wish they had a partner with their child's vitality, their finely tuned adaptation to their parent's inner life, and not the difficult work of relating to their actual partner or lack of one. Paradoxically, children can be obliged to be sacrificed to their parents' desires as the price to be paid for survival. The Oedipal configuration as conceived by Freud colludes in this sacrifice, turning a blind eye to the power imbalance of dependency and assigning responsibility to the child.

In fact, Freud began by locating covetous desire in the adults around a child, but drew back when he began to realize how widespread the phenomenon was. Case after case presented him with unacknowledged use of children by the adults around them. He reasoned that it could not therefore be true.

> One of Freud's earliest discoveries was that in the unconscious, memories and phantasies are not distinguished – hence his abandonment of his earliest theory of neurosis, the 'seduction' or 'affect trauma' theory. From that time onwards phantasies have been of central interest.
>
> (Bott Spillius, 2001)

Without the benefit of the neuroscience we now have available, Freud assumed that the overlap between what we remember and what we imagine meant that imagination invented memory. He realized that the mind does not distinguish, as Pally's (1997) work on memory later explains. On these grounds, he asserts that repressed unconscious processes 'equate reality of thought with external actuality, and wishes with their fulfilment – with the event' (Freud, 1911:225) This kind of concrete thinking – because we wish it, it must have happened, or, it happened because we wished it – tends to arise as a result of confusion between self and object, one of the consequences of projective identification (Segal, 1957) and a lack of triangulation.

Freud (1905) thought he must be seeing that Dora, for example, felt tremendous desire for the adults around her: for her father, her father's friend, and her father's mistress. He was unable to imagine that these adults used Dora for their own ends. In this, he may have been suffering from Steiner's (1985) blind eye: this is not something I (am prepared to) see. The blind eye implies its own recognition. In choosing this path, Freud was selectively ignoring classical wisdom on memory as re-membering, piecing together that which has been sundered, as in the myth of Osiris and Isis, in which Isis found the scattered pieces of her husband's body and bound them together.

Freud was also turning a blind eye to his teacher Janet's (1925) insight that the emotional intensity of traumatic events interferes with integration of the experience into existing memory schemes, causing them to be dissociated from consciousness, and to be stored instead as physiological sensations or visual images. This insight has been confirmed by twenty-first century neurobiology (van der Kolk et al., 2008) and can be confirmed every day in the mental health clinic (Mauritz et al., 2013).

What does this mean then for intergenerational, intrafamilial relations? Is there another way of conceptualizing the intrafamily dynamic that does not cast the child as perpetrator, albeit in phantasy? How can we face more squarely the power of the parent figures, their unmet need, that which is traumatic, unmediated in their own lives and passed on to their children? In response to a recent talk along these lines, someone remonstrated, sounding shocked: 'We cannot blame the parents'. No indeed. But can we bear instead to see unmet need unwittingly passed down? Perhaps we can move away from locating the badness in the child, and towards locating it in the way things felt. This is harder than it sounds; we do seem to need a representative for the badness. Even someone with Bion's insight would rather blame his child self, representing himself and not his childhood circumstances as difficult in his memoirs (1982), despite losing his ayah and his parents in being sent away as a young boy from the world he knew to boarding school in England. For the very fact of primal dependency, especially when dependency is a risky business, we cannot bite the hand that feeds us, and the reproach for harm done circles back on us. Bearing in mind that we are seeing a recreation of the qualities of a parent's or grandparent's early world helps in the attempt to move away from moralizing and from blame. Even cruelty, shocking as it is, speaks volumes about that early world. In moving towards new relational possibilities that include attempts to understand, though, there is a stumbling block; there is something primal in the need to seek a representation of the wrong, connected to a sense of how things should be, and 'a deep sense of order, justice and rightness', Alvarez's (2012:89) moral imperatives and rectifications.

The essential thing about psychoanalysis in its ideal is that it does not moralize, though society does, in the service of a system of social justice weighted on the side of the powerful, with which we as citizens largely comply. The Oedipal configuration as presently conceived holds us in thrall. Identity is the narrative by which we live our lives, the ground on which we stand. Our parents' view of us sets us on our path and writes the story of our lives. We are lucky indeed if our parents are free enough of their own childhoods not to visit them on us, and likewise our children. Who am I for you? is a useful question clinically, and also in problematic family relating. I am sometimes surprised that more is not made of the fact that Freud was not only allegedly self-analyzed, but also 'analyzed' his own daughter Anna, who lived her life carrying the torch into the future for Freud. Who was she for him, and thus for herself? I mentioned earlier that de Kesel (2017) reconceptualizes the Oedipal struggle as a struggle for identity, in which each of us have to both identify with and reject/be rejected by the parent. In order to organize these opposing flows of love and hate, to disentangle them for our own mental health, to have a sense of ourselves as both separate and connected, we have to be able to risk hating and being hated, as well as loving and being loved.

In clinical work with parents, questions of love, hate, power, and identity often take a while to surface consciously, but they are there from the beginning, as the following two stories show. I have chosen stories of adolescents, as this is a time when people are often beginning to question the terms on which they have lived their lives up until now. Seeds of depression planted in early childhood burst vividly into bloom. For twelve-year-old Kezia, and sixteen-year-old Leon, in being referred to child and adolescent mental health clinics, the assertion was that the disturbance was located in them, and not in their parents. However, it seems to me that each descriptor, or symptom, applied to the young person in their referral was at least as true of the parental relationship, particularly when the child was little. I will begin with Kezia's story.

Caught in the crossfire

Kezia's referral to a mental health clinic described her as 'unmanageable' and 'unstable' in school and at home. She was twelve years old and had the air of an actress in a modern-day soap opera, as if she was constructed from the outside. Indeed, she would sometimes gaze into a mirror and adopt kittenish 'selfie' poses, as if the camera was on her. Right at the beginning, her mother asked the therapist, 'Do you want me?' It was a question that felt freighted with disappointment. The feeling was of long-suffering exhausted resignation, and suggested an impossible choice. Never being given the chance to get away and do her own thing seemed equivalent to being wanted, but the alternative was to be rejected, excluded. She seemed to be communicating her own Oedipal struggle for identity in her opening question. To relate to her was to engage in oppression. Kezia was seen as the oppressor, and needed to comply in her own oppression (that of taking the role of oppressing her mother) in order to be present at all in her mother's scheme of things, her template for relating. This dynamic seems to represent a profound dilemma around identity: do you accept the version of yourself which negates you, or do you reject it, which negates a version of you but invites hostility? You can risk rejecting it and inviting hostility only if you have an ally: for example, one of your parents. If there is hostility in the parental relationship, the child between them can be caught in the crossfire. They can be used as a human shield, or a bullet. Either way, for the parent there is the satisfaction of seeing a difficult feeling expressed without fear of retaliation; it takes them out of the firing line. In an instance of the psychoanalytic concept of projective identification, a parent can put distance between themselves and the child embodying their aggression, distress, or confusion; thus detaching themselves from the difficult emotion.

In this way, Kezia, an only child, found herself not just the target but also the vehicle for resentment on behalf of both aggrieved parents. It cascaded down from long buried resentments at their parents, who for various reasons had not been able to see and support them as children. Kezia's mother needed someone – Kezia – to feel guilt about imposing servitude that her parents and her husband denied. Now that they had separated, Kezia was also a safe landing for her parents' frustration and fury with each other. No wonder she seemed to despair of ever really being seen, which manifested in a demand for total attention and a feeling of bottomless need, expressed sometimes as, 'I want everything!' Her fear of being left, of having nothing, seems to have led to an overclose relationship with her mother, which extended to sharing a bed at night and visiting the toilet together. It was a perfect arrangement in that her mother could experience Kezia's need to be physically close, to know where she is at all times, as tyrannical. In her daughter she had a safe target for resentment of the oppressor: 'Look what you're doing to me!' Kezia was not only overidentified with her mother, she was also preoccupied with her father. She would sleep in his bed when she stayed the night with him, ring him frequently, worry about him, and give him advice about his troubles.

Her behaviour in relation to her parents could be seen as Oedipally driven in the Freudian sense. Or we could see it as a desperate effort to be someone they each needed, to replace the missing people in their lives. It could be seen as driven by their need, rather than hers, a misuse of her, whether they knew it or not, whether they could help it or not. This is not about blame, it is about the relational way in which minds are made, about a child's search for an answer to the question of who she is. Kezia's father looked after her in her early days when her mother could not, at a rocky time for him personally, when the couple had already separated and he was under great emotional and relational pressure, ostracized by his family for his relationship with Kezia's mother, of whom they disapproved. Kezia conveyed a sense of her early world when in therapy sessions there gradually emerged what seemed like a very fragile and dissociated baby self. She would lie curled on the floor, rocking and humming in a detached, absent-minded, almost trance-like kind of way. Time seemed to crawl to a stop, and the world seemed to disappear. Her therapist sometimes felt on the verge of disappearing herself. Kezia was showing her how nobody was there. She was conveying through emotional resonance the story she could not tell of the way things were for her in the early days of her life. As her parents suffered and struggled and could not be really present for her, Kezia's brain had been building a million connections a second.

In contrast with these disappeared states of mind and body, there was at times a brittle brightness about Kezia, and a preoccupation with her looks. She insisted on a world in which everything was delightful and she was treasured. I think we have to be very careful in trying to understand such symptoms. The psychoanalytic framework sometimes seems to suggest that there is an innate factor, alongside a lack of parental containment, which rejects reality in favour of wish-fulfilment. Put it alongside parental absence of mind, though, and it begins to look like self-preservation. Nobody in Kezia's world was looking to take responsibility for, to take on the work of responding to her state of mind. For all kinds of reasons, sometimes obliviously absorbed in the intensity of their fights, her parents behaved as though she was not there. The truth was, Kezia needed to join them in rejecting her reality if she wanted to forge any kind of bond with them. Her reality was sometimes a painful one in which things were not as she would wish them to be, and no one in her everyday life was available to triangulate this perception. In Britton's (1998) terms, her therapist offered another perspective to help her become aware of perceptions as beliefs rather than concrete facts. In this way, I think the very value of child psychotherapy can be problematic if there is no opportunity for concurrent work with parents. It risks putting children outside the frame of a family dynamic in which they carry the problem. There was evidence of this when towards the end of Kezia's therapy, a very real worry surfaced about stepping out of the alternative framework that therapy offered, without the protection, however illusory, that her bright bubble world had offered.

The complex constellation of parent-child relationships, carrying the charge of previous generations, structures our very thinking (Hobson, 2002), shapes our interactions with the world and so contours the world we live in. How can we separate out the child's desires from the parents', the child's identity from the way in which he has been seen or unseen, a screen for projection of untold stories? The attribution of characteristics is tangled with who the parents feel themselves and each other to be, in the light of their own early experience. This seemed to be true of Kezia's story, and also of Leon's, to which I will now turn. In Leon's family, identity was problematic, and the identity problem was located in him.

The family setup

Sixteen-year-old Leon had recently taken an overdose and was referred to a mental health clinic, where the family met with a therapist. His parents, Angela and Kevin, were buzzing in excited agitation as they reported a psychiatrist having told Leon he thought he was special, and needed to come down a peg or two. There was a feeling of being united in vindication, even gratified, as if he had got his come-uppance. It seemed to be strikingly hard for them to think about the urgency of the suicide attempt, let alone where the feeling of being special had come from, though it gradually became clear over a series of meetings that Leon had been made to feel 'special' in a number of ways. Not only his mother but his grandmother too had turned to him and wanted him to stay overnight with her during difficulties in her marriage. There was a sense that he was held to blame for having been used in this way.

In terms of an Oedipal dynamic, from behaviour alone it certainly could have looked as if there was an impulse to replace his father with his mother in her bed, but this impulse did not seem to belong to Leon in the way that Freud's theory suggests. It felt more as though he was accepting the only kind of closeness on offer in the absence of the boundaried, attuned, comforting relationship he needed. Talking of children's need for a parent in terms of sexuality obscures more than it reveals; dependency and the need for responsive, contingent connection are missing from this account. Harlow's (1958) monkeys show that comforting contact is essential to the psychological development of infants. Maternal comfort was hard to access in the turbulence of Angela and Kevin's relationship, and their relationship with Leon, who was born when was a teenager. A dynamic between the three of them held sway that prioritized sexuality and often exemplified the storms of adolescence.

Leon's overdose seemed to represent his response to an impossible dilemma: if these are the terms on which I am special, I would rather not be here. It did not feel possible for the couple to talk with him about the roots of the special feeling. It was a given, an accepted fact that could not be thought about as a belief, and therefore they could not think about whose belief it might be. It may not even have 'belonged' (in so far as feelings ever belong) to Leon's parents' generation. Kevin's rather furtive, hunted demeanour conveyed a feeling of not measuring up. It seemed there may have been something or someone seen as not lived up to in his birth family, weak or deficient in some way. Leon seemed to be required to be the person living up to whatever was missing, and to take responsibility for associated difficulties, too.

Contempt has a long history, and trickles down the generations, corroding all in its path. There was certainly contempt around in this family, and Leon was experienced as the source of it. Angela would talk tearfully about the dreadful things he said. She said Leon thought he was the man. He was represented as having the power, and she backed Leon against Kevin if there was a conflict, as a way of humiliating him. So there was a horrible satisfaction in the arrangement as it stood, in which both parents played out long-standing grievances in relation to Leon, reinforcing their sense of what they had suffered by recreating it in the present. Much of what went on in the family seemed to be co-opted into communicating propaganda for a marital public relations war. I will look more closely at the nature of grievance in the chapter 'Getting your own back: Revisiting resistance', but suffice it to say here that there was not much sign of any investment in change for Leon's family. Quite the reverse, in fact, as they were receiving a carer's allowance now for Leon. His symptoms were bringing some money into the family, which played into the role imbalance, as his father was not then in work. Kevin could be taunted about it, but could not challenge it, and may have even been grateful too.

It would be long slow work to try to triangulate the impact that each parent's individual experiences of childhood, horrible in different ways, had on the way things were between the three of them. I draw on this family story to show how far from Leon's experience might be the idea that he wanted to sleep with his mother. If we are to avoid collusion with a denial of the power imbalance and consequent problematization of the child, the Oedipus complex needs reframing in the light of the unconscious use of the child by their parents to re-present the unacknowledged pain of their own childhoods.

Leon understood himself as there to support his mother, to be at different times the kind of sibling, mother, and man that were missing from her life. He also needed to be the backstop for his father and the rest of the family, the clever one who sorts things out when no one knows what to do. He then had to take in the parental reproach for his temerity in being 'above himself'. This perfectly prevented Angela and Kevin from the difficult effort of being the parents they needed to be for him, and also usefully provided them with someone to join up against. The extremity of his confusion about where to put himself, who to be, seems inevitable, given this family context. He has had to embody necessary figures for his parents, who would themselves otherwise be in an impossible position. I will think more about missing people and identity in the next chapter, but here would like to note that Leon's parents have essentially exported into him the profoundly disturbing – unliveable – conflict of being their parent while being their child, in order to be able to continue their lives and maintain a degree of stability in a relatively uncomplicated way. Their stance towards him seemed to say, 'It's not us; it's him'.

His suicidality expresses the absolutely conflicting and confusional nature of the missing people he was required to be in his family, aspects of intergenerational relationships both longed for and actual, internalized as aspects of his identity: the good father/partner to his mother and grandmother, rescuing the women from the men; the contemptuous father, humiliating his son/father and his mother, too; the teenage ally to his teenage mother; the clever father/son who sorts things out but lords it over the rest of the family. His confusion is brought to the clinic to be medicated, because it is essential for the continuation of the family system that he undertakes these conflicting roles. That is how this particular Oedipus was framed.

In thinking about the symptoms for which children and adolescents like Kezia and Leon are brought to a clinic to be treated and even medicated, it is high time we took into account the relational way in which minds are made and identities become established. We can no longer turn a blind eye towards the power balance of dependency. Seeing children's and adolescents' symptoms as personal attributes rather than reflecting relational experience in the intergenerational family system becomes itself symptomatic of a troubling disavowal. It seems relevant in relation to this problematic dynamic to turn now to think more about how the presence of absence manifests in our lives, so that we come to embody qualities in people we may never have known.

References

Alvarez, A. (2012). *The Thinking Heart: Three levels of psychoanalytic therapy with disturbed children*. London: Routledge.

Baldwin, J. (1965). *Cambridge Debate: Has the American Dream Been Achieved at the Expense of the American Negro?* Retrieved from www.youtube.com/watch?v=nbkObXxSUus.

Bauer, A., Parsonage, M., Knapp, M., Lemmi, V., & Adelaja, B. (2014). *The Costs of Perinatal Mental Health Problems*. Personal Social Services Research Unit & the Centre for Mental Health. Retrieved from http://eprints.lse.ac.uk/59885/.

Bion, W. R. (1982). In F. Bion (Ed.), *The Long Weekend: 1897–1919 (part of a Life)*. Fleetwood: Abingdon.

Bott Spillius, E. (2001). Freud and Klein on the concept of phantasy. *International Journal of Psycho-Analysis*, 82(2):361–374.

Britton, R. (1989). The missing link: Parental sexuality in the Oedipus complex. In R. Britton, M. Feldman, & E. O'Shaughnessy (Eds.), *The Oedipus Complex Today: Clinical Implications*. London: Karnac, 83–101.

Britton, R. (1998). *Belief and Imagination: Explorations in Psychoanalysis*. London: Routledge.

de Kesel, M. (2017). Identity: Modernity's real myth. *Paper presented at European Meeting of the International Society for the Psychoanalytical Study of Organizations*. Amsterdam, March, 2017.

Freud, S. (1905). Fragment of an analysis of a case of hysteria. In J. Strachey (Ed. & Trans.), *The Standard Edition of the Complete Psychological Works of Sigmund Freud*, Vol. 7:7–122. London: Hogarth.

Freud, S. (1909). Little Hans. Two case histories. In J. Strachey (Ed.), *The Standard Edition of the Complete Psychological Works of Sigmund Freud*, Vol. 10:3–147. London: Hogarth.

Freud, S. (1911). Formulations on the two principles of mental functioning. In J. Strachey (Ed.), *The Standard Edition of the Complete Psychological Works of Sigmund Freud*, Vol. 12:213–226. London: Hogarth.

Harlow, H. F. (1958). The nature of love. *American Psychologist*, 13:673–685.
Hobson, P. (2002). *The Cradle of Thought*. London: Macmillan.
Janet, P. (1925). H. M. Guthrie & E. R. Guthrie (Trans.), *Principles of Psychotherapy*. London: Allen & Unwin.
Jones, A. (2006). How video can bring to view pathological defensive processes and facilitate the creation of triangular space in perinatal parent–Infant psychotherapy. *Infant Observation: International Journal of Infant Observation & Its Applications*, 9(2):109–123.
Joyce, J. (1975). Letter to Harriet Shaw Weaver, 1926. In R. Ellmann (Ed.), *Selected Letters of James Joyce*. London: Faber, 318.
Klein, M. (1932). *The Psycho-analysis of Children*. New York: Norton.
Larkin, P. (2018). Letter to Monica Jones, August 1968. In J. Booth (Ed.), *Philip Larkin: Letters Home, 1936–77*. London: Faber, 390.
Mauritz, M. W., Goossens, P. J. J., Draijer, N., & van Achterberg, T. (2013). Prevalence of interpersonal trauma exposure and trauma-related disorders in severe mental illness. *European Journal of Psychotraumatology*, 4:10–25 Retrieved from doi:10.3402/ejpt.v4i0.19985.
Pally, R. (1997). Memory: Brain systems that link past, present and future. *International Journal of Psychoanalysis*, 78(6):1223–1234.
Segal, H. (1957). Notes on symbol formation. *International Journal of Psycho-Analysis*, 38:391–397.
Steiner, J. (1985). Turning a blind eye: The cover up for Oedipus. *International Review of Psychoanalysis*, 12:161–172.
van der Kolk, B. A., Hopper, J., & Osterman, J. E. (2008). Exploring the nature of traumatic memory. *Journal of Aggression, Maltreatment & Trauma*, 4 (2):9–31.

Chapter 4

Missing people

The presence of absence

Psychoanalysis has much to teach about missing people and identity. Many of its core insights into the undercurrents of human behaviour are substantiated by modern developmental research, though there has been a real shift of emphasis in recent years from individual to mutual construction of meaning. In this chapter, I revisit Freud's ideas about mourning and melancholia, or what we might now call clinical depression, in terms of relational development. I look at the impact of the presence of absence: what happens when we cannot acknowledge loss of vital supports we may never really have had. We will consider ways in which unacknowledged loss makes itself felt, so that an unsuffered loss can itself be a presence, with its own ways of being.

In writing about chronic depression, Freud (1917) describes the emotion as akin to that of mourning, a longing for something lost. The loss feels vividly present, embodied, yet oddly unknown. Like a fish in water, you cannot see it because you are in it; it is one of the conditions of your existence. My sense is that what is missing is an awareness of the relation to the lost thing. Instead there is the concrete roadblock of what Segal (1957) has called a symbolic equation, preventing forward travel. The idea here is of something re-presented, made present again as if actually, rather than symbolically represented through a mediating mind. The terms of relating are different: in the first, they are predetermined, the script is already written and ad libs are ignored; in the second, we are free to improvise, and take the conversation anywhere we like. In melancholia, the possibility of negotiation around the psychic roadblock is deleted from awareness, and with it the degree of distance, of perspective, which might offer other possible imaginative avenues. Taking this idea further: when we feel suicidal, something needs to die, but it may not be us. It may be a pre-set pattern of relating that has been imposed upon us, a relationship to somebody long gone whom we have been unwittingly used to re-present. In this sense suicidality can paradoxically mean fighting for your life, although it is a fight to the death. We will consider three vivid conflicts finding expression in stories of suicidality later in the chapter, but will look first at what lies behind the thick grey veil of depression.

Depressive symptoms express a lack of self-care, a washed-out unwillingness to get out of bed and go on. There is a withdrawal of consent for the prevailing terms of engagement. On this basis, life feels untenable. Depression can thus be seen as an expression of the need to renegotiate the terms on which someone lives their life. From this perspective, the severity of the stretch of depression would depend upon how negotiable those terms are felt to be. If it is almost impossible to imagine and explore other possible ways of being, if they can be glimpsed but are felt to be out of reach or behind a glass wall, no wonder there is despair. Despair feels quite healthy in these circumstances, and I have often found myself encouraging people not to waste a good breakdown. At other times, though, it is not possible to be so glib. If a child has been used to re-present something missing, an unthinkable and unresolved loss in the parent's life, as we will see in some of the stories that follow, the chances of renegotiation can seem to be nil. Sometimes there has been an absolute one-to-one equation of the missing quality and the child. The very idea of a conversation around identity may itself be missing. Depression then persists through adolescence long into adulthood, often to the sad confusion of the person experiencing its heavy downward pull. Without the possibility of conversation offered by another perspective, however far away, I am trapped in someone's identification of me. Paradoxically, the only way out is suicide.

The attributed identification is unquestioned, unquestionable, in the context of the family system. In what follows I would like to relate this to the experience of loss, and what we do about missing something we cannot afford to lose. Some of the children's stories we have thought about so far seem to teach us that we seek to re-present the people we cannot bear to miss. The paradoxical tragedy is that the degree to which we cannot bear to miss someone is the degree to which they were never really there for us.

To internalize a relationship, indeed to have a relationship, there must be a degree of distance, an awareness of two separate beings, and of the imaginative link between the two that survives separation.

Essentially, if it is mediated (in Freudian terms, installed in the ego) the relationship to it can continue even when the physical presence is gone. On the other hand, when our relationship to the missing person is unmediated by an available attuned mind, when it is not possible to be aware of the relationship, we have what Bick (1968) called adhesive identification, a kind of 'I am here when I am stuck to you' state of mind, which persists as long as physical presence is available. Absence equals abandonment – if you are gone, I am gone. Solitude becomes a kind of annihilation. The solution is to hallucinate the missing person, to embody them, or seek to re-present them. Not represent, which would imply a symbolic link, a mediating mind, but re-present, make present through the kind of illusory identification that the precarious nature of the connection made necessary.

The prospect of losing something we have never really had is excruciatingly painful, involving as it does losing the possibility of hope that it will one day materialize. I think we keep that hope alive by refusing to acknowledge the unbearable loss: we embody the missing person, or we choose someone else to re-present them. Children offer an ideal (though unconscious) choice for their parents, because their identity is malleable, and emerges through the ways of being of the primary relationship.

In order to illuminate this process of re-presenting missing people, before we turn to some stories that exemplify this painful process, I will consider some of Freud's groundbreaking ideas about the mind and unconscious experience.

Repression and the received version of events

Before the twentieth century began, Freud had realized that the language of a mental illness drew its vocabulary, its symptoms, from emotionally charged experience. A girl who had had to nurse her father, putting his leg across her lap to change his bandage every day, came to Freud with pains beginning at the very spot on her thigh where her father's leg had rested. From then on 'her painful legs began to "join in the conversation" during our analyses' (Breuer & Freud, 1895:141), the body expressing what the mind could not bear. Freud tended to see the emotional charge of what the mind cannot bear in terms of sexual desire, but the case for sex as the arch motivator of repression is worth reconsidering. In considering the case above, for example, it is quite possible to see resentment about nursing her father as inadmissible in the family system, not compatible with goodness, and therefore in need of repression in the girl's idea of herself. Her symptom expressed what was unsayable in the family story, which in turn forms the basis for her identity, as contemporary researchers like Stern (1985) have shown. The roots of repression can be seen to be relational: there are truths that cannot find expression in the received version of the story, and the body re-presents them.

The emotional impact of a whole range of human experience is expressed in the body, especially that which cannot be acknowledged in the relationships on which we depend. Like a choir, our cells sing out about what we have been through. Our voices cannot speak that which cannot find representation in the mind, but our bodies tell the story – or keep the score, as van der Kolk puts it (2014). Another way of describing the repressed is that which cannot find representation in another mind and thence in our own. The point is not (only) that we cannot bear the existence of these emotional countercurrents, it is that the original mind-forming relationship could not bear them.

This relational process of giving voice to meaning underpins psychoanalysis. Here the therapeutic relationship bears the weight of feelings transferred onto the therapist, who receives them as a communication about relational experience. Meaning is sought for the re-presentation of physiological experience (expressed as a symptom) in the therapeutic relationship, in order for it to find representation in the mind. The quality of the psychoanalyst's attentive receptiveness transforms a physical symptom into a mental quality, much as Winnicott's 'ordinary, devoted mother' (1957) receives her baby's terror and translates it through understanding into something that can be apprehended in the mind. It can be represented by the word 'hungry', say. Inevitably, the word for the thing depends on the mother's own experience in her family, social, and cultural context. A mother with a reasonably good experience of being looked after might recognize hunger and call it that, but another mother who did not have a good experience of early care may understand her baby's screaming not as hunger but as anger, for example. If she already feels worthless, the screaming may feel like confirmation. She can feel that the baby hates her, and she is bad mother, or perhaps she feels that the baby is a persecuting monster. Either way, it does not turn out well for the baby, who has no other way of understanding his impulses. The emotions on his mother's face and in her voice are his guide to reality; more than that, they are his reality.

For good or ill, then, we are understood by our parents in the context of their own experience of relationships – how else are they to understand us? Their terms of reference for understanding us are themselves established through relating, as we have seen. For each of us, the Oedipal frame that we considered in the previous chapter, the world of our parents' relationship with each other and with us, establishes the ground we stand on. What is known and knowable in that world can be expressed in the received version of events; what is unacknowledged, unknowable, is redacted from the account. It is expressed through the body in the return of the repressed.

Freud's emphasis on sexuality as the vital force in repression may shed some light on his own social and relational context. Freud's friend Fliess had some rather eccentric ideas about sexuality, and from their letters it seems that Freud was influenced by his thinking. Freud, being human, was not exempt from the anticipation machine of the mind (Siegel, 1999) and like the rest of us, was bound to find what he already knew. Long before he wrote his great paper on mourning and melancholia, in conversation with Fliess we see the germ of the ideas:

> The neurosis concerned with eating, parallel to melancholia, is anorexia. The famous anorexia nervosa of young girls seems to me (on careful observation) to be a melancholia where sexuality is undeveloped. The patient asserted that she had not eaten, simply because she had no appetite, and for no other reason. Loss of appetite – in sexual terms – loss of libido.
>
> (Freud, 1895:99)

We can hear the delight in Freud's summative logic, but there are all kinds of other possible theories about not eating. Harlow (1958) found that the comfort of others was key: baby monkeys who were isolated for three months refused to eat and died of what he called 'emotional anorexia'. The effect of Freud's logic in making an absolute association with sexuality is of material fitting a theory that had already begun to form in his mind. In other circumstances he does not take the word of the patient as sacrosanct in quite this way; here perhaps the words fit his preconception.

However, much of the force of what Freud says in *Studies in Hysteria* (1895) is that mental illness speaks to us in body language, conveying thoughts that have to be secret, because they cannot yet find expression in language. As Hobson (2002) explains in *The Cradle of Thought*, the roots of language, of thinking, lie in relation to our earliest caregiver. When our impulses have not found expression in language in this relationship, they do not become thoughts, because there is no mental representation; they are instead experiences outside the scope of awareness. Indeed, as we saw for Aisha, Adam, Kezia, and Leon, and as I will try to show in Maria, Shaun, and Clare's stories shortly, the equilibrium of the family system may require that these experiences stay outside awareness. Furthermore, if family assumptions mean that a child has to be ill, focus on the child's symptoms and not the family system that necessitated them means that parents avoid the difficult work of recovery, which would involve their own painful relinquishing of the hope of a better past.

Making a better past

The story of Maria, the daughter of a refugee, comes to mind, who struggled in successive schools with constant worries and grievances about friends and teachers. She would come home each day and relate her troubles to her father, who was eager to hear them and to swing into action on her behalf. Nothing but a school move would do, until life at that school too became unendurable. As the family history emerged, it shed light on this mystifying process. It became clear that what her father was doing in rescuing his daughter was rescuing his mother, whom he had been unable to protect as a young boy in a country at war. It was vital that Maria continue to experience as much suffering as she could, so that he could step in and be the active protector that he still longed to be for the mother he lost many years ago.

It seems to me that this and other stories of the attempt to make a better past show how entangled our sense of identity can be with that of other generations we may never have known. The confusion that arises when we are unwittingly identified with a missing person in the family is profoundly connected with our mental health. Maria's sense of seeking to find something very wrong in rather ordinary situations, made her seem mad to those who did not know the family story, which included Maria herself. She had come to know that there was something very wrong, and that in some confused way, she was identified with it, and her closeness to her father depended upon it. When such a sad relational truth is looking for redress, and it finds expression in the next generation, the identification can to some extent be rejected or claimed, depending on other relational possibilities, chiefly the presence or absence of an ally. Maria's mother was potentially in a position to offer another perspective, but she was herself frightened and confused by the enactment she witnessed, and had no way of understanding it. Once she did begin to see the dynamic as part of family history, she would have had to step outside her husband's frame of reference to challenge it, and she did not feel the relationship was strong enough to withstand it. When things are shaky and there is no ally in sight, claiming the identification as Maria did may seem to offer a way of shoring up a precarious connection, but at the cost of profound disconnection with self-experience.

This seemed to be the case for Adam, the boy I mentioned in the chapter 'Behaviour as communication: do you get me?' who was suffering from an eating disorder. He was scarily thin when he was discharged from hospital on the understanding he came to an eating disorder clinic. The trouble turned out not to be about the food. He could not talk about a trauma he had suffered as a young child when his father, with whom he was identified in the family, killed himself. His self-starvation seemed to be a way of carrying his father with him, of making a claim on his identity. He embodied his father's suicidality until such time as he could begin to bear to approach the grim experience of his tragic loss. Until then, he offered his body to re-present his father in the family. I think he may have been seeking to find himself in his state of mind, facing self-inflicted death as he was. It was perhaps his way of keeping him close, and keeping him present in his mother's mind, too. He could not bear to lose him, although he already had.

What happens then when we cannot afford to lose someone, especially someone we have never really had, is that we embody them. This means of course, that we cannot mourn them. There is an absence of loss, instead the presence of absence makes itself felt. Very often, we seem to need to rely on applying Freud's 'patch over the place where originally a rent had appeared in the ego's relation to the external world' (Freud, 1924:151). Part of what I am suggesting in this chapter is that our children, like Maria, can be used to provide this patch over the tear in our sense of ourselves.

Perhaps for this reason among others, parents do not necessarily welcome changes for the better in their children. It seems that the troubling symptom might offer a way of relating to feelings that could not otherwise belong in the story we want to tell ourselves, the story about ourselves that we can live with. I will now turn back to Aisha's story, in which her symptoms seemed to offer a way of locating and regulating maternal distress and anxiety, and consider links between this idea and the presence of absence in her mother's life.

Missing hero

Trying to understand what the world was like for Aisha, as a way of building a relationship that could help regulate her states of mind and body, involved understanding her mother's losses. Like any child, Aisha played a part in the family system, representing unacknowledged states of mind. Some of these were qualities experienced in relation to the people her mother was missing but could not mourn. This process is at least as much inevitable as pathological. The interpersonal way in which minds develop means that Aisha could only be understood by her mother in relation to the world to which she herself is adapted. She understood her ways of being through drawing on her own emotional repertoire, depending on the risks and opportunities felt to be around in her own formative early world.

In her play in therapy, Aisha began to convey something of what it was like for her to be in this particular world. Once, an engine she was playing with fell off the table, dragging its trucks down too. She immediately wanted to leave. Her mother, Anita, gave a nervous warning look, and said she had had a meltdown about this already. Presumably she meant Aisha had had the meltdown, but the way she put it is instructive. It was hard to know whose feelings they were, or who was more frightened of being overwhelmed. Anita said they had lost Aisha's engine, Hero, and could not find a new one. This struck home as a powerful symbol in both of their emotional lives. As well as an overwhelmed mother with unresolved trauma, Aisha had a father who lived abroad, and could neither be present in her life nor be her mother's partner in regulation. In her play, Aisha conveyed a sense of her lived experience, which inevitably related to her mother's experience: rescue was desperately needed, and a Hero was missing.

The symptoms Aisha expressed were on behalf of a family context in which major losses meant there was not often an available parental mind to think about her struggles and worries. Rather, she found sometimes a mind overwhelmed by actual and potential difficulties, and itself desperately needing attention. There was such a tangle of feelings that it was hard to say who was communicating whose. To locate symptoms in the child, to see them as essentially belonging to the child in circumstances like this seems misguided, at the very least. In Aisha's case, things got better as therapy went on, as long as her mother had recourse to an available mind in therapy sessions of her own. Aisha's equanimity improved as together she and her therapist found ways of expressing some of the feeling of what happened.

Although therapeutic work with Aisha did seem to lead to steps forward in some spheres, this was not a source of relief for her mother; quite the reverse. Improvements seemed to be regarded as unhelpful disconfirmations of her experience. In a kind of 'see-saw' phenomenon, Anita became increasingly troubled during this time. Aisha's improvement meant that she was no longer the presenting symptom for the family, the symptom which makes present the unspoken difficulties, lying under the surface. These began to be uncovered by the receding tide of Aisha's dyregulated emotional state, and I think her mother felt exposed and ashamed. Aisha's rage had become present-day evidence of the thing Anita feared. In a sense, Anita was gathering evidence for the prosecution, a process that may lie behind the clinical notion of resistance, which we will consider in more detail in the next chapter. It seemed that Anita needed a witness more than she needed a solution. She needed the trouble to continue to re-present what she was up against, until someone got it. In her own separate therapy, once someone got the disturbance, felt the force of it and began to think about what it was like for her, she could begin to establish some representation of it in her mind and develop a new relationship to it. This process, though, is not without its losses, and we will go on to think more about them in the next chapter.

You will see that I am trying to illustrate here the distinction I have mentioned between re-presentation as enactment in the present, entailing embodied unmediated experience, a symptom in search of a mind, and representation, where the disturbing experience has been witnessed, felt, and acknowledged. It is received by somebody and given symbolic representation, in a facial expression, or a gesture, or emotionally resonant words, so that it can be taken in by the person concerned in a new form, with added understanding. The very process of connecting in a new way, and opening up new kinds of communication through the new connection, means that Schutz's (2005) red phone of emotionality can be answered in a regulating way. Seeking meaning reduces the sense of alarm and intrusion. The communication can now be thought about from a range of perspectives, rather than concretely embodied.

This communicative connection arises through a relationship which acknowledges qualities as distinct from people, which can look at things from another point of view. To put it another way, and link it with psychoanalytic thinking and the previous chapter, it is the result of Britton's (1989) missing link and a secure Oedipal constellation. If your parents can think about what happens to you, and how you feel about it, you can take in a way of understanding your own experience that includes the capacity to think about what happens to you. If they themselves are preoccupied and cannot take in your experience, you can only continue to embody it, along with the feeling that nobody really gets it, and also, to a greater or lesser degree, the desire to get your own back.

For Aisha, the maternal response to the missing hero seems to be a significant factor in shaping her identity. What if Aisha had been chosen by her mother to represent the heroic and not its absence? Something more like this seems to have been the case for Freud. In 1885, long before his rise to prominence, Freud was writing to his future wife about frustrating his biographers:

> Let them worry, we have no desire to make it easy for them. Each one of them will be right in his opinion of "The Development of the Hero", and I am already looking forward to seeing them go astray.
>
> (Freud, 1885/1960:141)

Another first son of a much younger second wife came to a mental health clinic at six years old on a rather different trajectory. He was referred for anxiety and aggressive, disruptive behaviour. His mother was small and childlike, and seemed to be relying on her son Shaun for comfort and protection at that time because her husband was in prison. Shaun wore wrestling gear to his appointments and spent quite a bit of time shoving all the finger puppets into a cage and blockading them in. It did not take a psychoanalytic education to see that he was scared, and that for him, it was not safe to be soft and small. No wonder he came out fighting. Children who have witnessed domestic violence as he had are scarred (and often scared) for life. Even when they respond to fear by identifying with the aggressor (A. Freud, 1937), as a safer thing to do, the fear is still in their body. What is more, they have seen their caregiver as a perpetrator of violence, or as unable to protect themselves from it. Having a frightened or frightening caregiver makes for fear without resolution; there is no safe place to run if things are dangerous. The child's developing system finds nobody there to answer the red phone's urgent call and connect in a regulating way. No wonder this young boy's behaviour was aggressive and disruptive; he was showing us an aggressive, disruptive world of relating, in which he could find no sanctuary.

Rather, he was supposed to be the missing protector. It seems crass and cruel to see Shaun as the problem, and try to somehow 'treat' him out of his fear and attempts at self-protection, without reference to the context of domestic violence and its enduring impact.

Fairbairn (1946) was one of the first psychoanalytic thinkers to focus on relationships rather than individuals. I mentioned earlier his idea of the child experiencing emotional responsiveness from his parents as goodness and unresponsiveness as badness. His thinking opens up a far-reaching and neurobiologically valid way of thinking about responsive development in a relational context. This suggests Freud's insight that the shadow of the object falls upon the ego might apply to qualities of relating, that which is conveyed in and through relating. Phillips, who has edited Freud's oeuvre, writes that it seems 'entirely plausible to imagine that parents convey far more than they intend, and that children take in, in whatever form, far more than the parents or the children suspect' (2002:203). In understanding what symptoms communicate, then, it seems sensible to take into account what has been taken in implicitly.

The presence of absence

This was the case for Clare, who was referred for psychotherapy shortly before her eighteenth birthday because she felt suicidal. On the threshold of independence, she was actively considering ways of ending her life. As one possible factor among others, it emerged that she had undergone surgery as a very small child, and there was still a three-year-old girl in her parents' minds who was vulnerable after an operation and could not face the world. In this version of her, she needed to be kept at home and protected from other people and even from being outside. Her parents acknowledged the continuing force of this idea of their daughter, and it seemed to link with some of her seemingly self-limiting behaviours and a resistance to the idea of her being strong, active, and capable. In the terms of the thinking explored in this chapter, her parents' holding onto that idea is likely to be linked to an unacknowledged loss. In fact it became apparent that Clare's grandmother had died when her mother was three. In all the pain, loss, and confusion, there had been a period when nobody was available to look after Clare's mother as a little girl. She seemed now to have located the needs of that long ago three-year-old in her daughter, and embodied the missing person herself. Attending to her own need, located in her daughter, kept alive the hope that someone was coming.

Facing her own loss meant acknowledging that no one was coming, which felt like a cruel and painful abandonment of her own three-year-old self. Re-presenting the past in this way, though, prevented her from responding to her daughter's own actual needs in the present.

This paradigm made sense of Clare's feeling that suicide was a brave thing to do. She was sparing her mother the pain of realizing her daughter wanted to leave home and stand on her own two feet. Furthermore, suicide had the advantage of evading the ruthlessness that she was scared to find in herself; that of having her own thoughts and feelings, quite separate from her mother, and possibly in opposition to her. If she directed her hostility towards her own self, she need not direct the full force of her outrage at her virtual imprisonment against her mother, whom she feared would not survive such an attack. Punishing herself with self harm or even death seemed to her to be a reasonable thing to do in this state of mind. Her feeling was that it would also be an exciting, daring thing to do, as if continuing to live would be, among other things, a cop-out. On the only terms she knew, in a sense it was, in that it complied with her mother's project: she could continue to embody her mother's tragic loss, and be the focus of the caring support her mother needed to offer.

Clare was able to begin to think with a therapist about this state of mind, while parallel sessions were made available to her parents. Eventually, her mother was able to grieve the loss of her own mother, and the idea of a different path seemed to open up for Clare. It took a slow, careful piecing together of the missing people in the puzzle of their family life for this path to come into view.

Perhaps in this consideration of depression and suicidality as the embodiment of missing people, we are really thinking about what we cannot leave behind in arriving in the present moment. How could Maria's father leave behind the hope of alleviating his mother's suffering? Or Aisha's mother, or Clare's, the hope of someone coming to their rescue? Maybe we never really leave states of mind behind, but carry them with us, more or less consciously, in physical symptoms, or patterns of relating. Perhaps 'forgetting' is really a way of carrying it with us, lodged in the body. It seems that something like this process may happen for nation states too, if we consider the bleak poverty and deprivation left behind/carried with emigrants from many European countries in arriving at the 'American dream'. The hallucinated experience is that of the triumph of the self-made man, denying the suffering of generations that have gone before. Leader's (2016) biography of Saul Bellow tells of a generation of fathers surviving pogroms and managing to get to the United States, but raging at their sons for the ease of their lives. A new perspective on the Oedipal configuration is thus brought into being: how can a child be forgiven what he has not had to suffer?

In as many ways as there are potentialities for experience, unconscious relational memories are carried forward. What Bollas calls the 'unthought known' or the 'maternal aesthetic' (1987:32) is neurobiologically validated by the development research of the past three decades. It is expressed in patterns of relating. We take in the ways of apprehending the world that show in our mother's face and in the expressive movement of her body; her patterns of vitality and her emotionality conveying unspoken instructions about who we are and how we live. What we have gone through continues to go through us, whether we know it or not. Our parents' unresolved losses are expressed in us, just as we in the next generation locate the people we cannot afford to miss in our children, and our relation to them.

References

Bick, E. (1968). The experience of the skin in early object relations. *International Journal of Psychoanalysis*, 49:184–186.

Bollas, C. (1987). *The Shadow of the Object: Psychoanalysis of the Unthought Known*. London: Free Association.

Breuer, J. & Freud, S. (1895). Studies in hysteria. In J. Strachey (Ed. & Trans.), *The Standard Edition of the Complete Psychological Works of Sigmund Freud*, Vol. 2:1–335. London: Hogarth.

Britton, R. (1989). The missing link: Parental sexuality in the Oedipus complex. In R. Britton, M. Feldman, & E. O'Shaughnessy (Eds.), *The Oedipus Complex Today: Clinical Implications*. London: Karnac, 83–101.

Fairbairn, W. R. D. (1946). Object-relationships and dynamic structure. *International Journal of Psychoanalysis*, 27:30–37.

Freud, A. (1937). Identification with the Aggressor. In *The Ego and Mechanisms of Defence*. London: Karnac.

Freud, S. (1895). Draft G: Extracts from the Fliess papers. In J. Strachey (Ed. & Trans.), *The Standard Edition of the Complete Psychological Works of Sigmund Freud*, Vol. 1:263–266. London: Hogarth.

Freud, S. (1917). Mourning and Melancholia. In J. Strachey (Ed. & Trans.), *The Standard Edition of the Complete Psychological Works of Sigmund Freud*, Vol. 14:237–260. London: Hogarth.

Freud, S. (1924). Neurosis and psychosis. In J. Strachey (Ed.), *The Standard Edition of the Complete Psychological Works of Sigmund Freud*, Vol. 19:147–153. London: Hogarth.

Freud, S. (1960). Letter to Martha Bernhays, 1885. In E. L. Freud (Ed.), *Letters of Sigmund Freud, 1873–1939*:142–143. New York: Basic.

Harlow, H. F. (1958). The nature of love. *American Psychologist*, 13:673–685.

Hobson, P. (2002). *The Cradle of Thought*. London: Macmillan.

Leader, Z. (2016). *The Life of Saul Bellow, Volume 1: To Fame and Fortune, 1915–1964*. NY: Vintage.

Phillips, A. (2002). *Promises, Promises: Essays on Literature and Psychoanalysis*. London: Faber & Faber.

Schutz, L. E. (2005). Broad-perspective perceptual disorder of the right hemisphere. *Neuropsychology Review*, 15:11–27.

Segal, H. (1957). Notes on symbol formation. *International Journal of Psycho-Analysis*, 38:391–397.

Siegel, D. J. (1999). *The Developing Mind: Toward a Neurobiology of Interpersonal Experience*. New York: Guilford.

Stern, D. (1985). *The Interpersonal World of the Infant: A View from Psychoanalysis and Developmental Psychology*. New York: Basic.

van der Kolk, B. A. (2014). *The Body Keeps the Score: Brain, Mind, and Body in the Healing of Trauma*. New York: Penguin.

Winnicott, D. W. (1957). The ordinary devoted mother and her baby. In J. Hardenberg (Ed.), *The Child and the Family*. London: Tavistock. (Original work published 1949), 3–47.

Chapter 5

Getting your own back

Revisiting resistance

There is talk in the UK at the time of writing about separating from Europe; one impetus seems to be an idea of getting our own back, of regaining what was lost. Such a move implies a 'them and us' polarity in a number of ways; it would, for example, necessitate a European border in Ireland between north and south. Until the Good Friday agreement was signed in 1998 of course, there was such a border in Ireland, because of troubles arising from the colonizing of Ireland by the English hundreds of years ago. The conflict that came out of this has cost many lives on both sides, people dying to right wrongs inflicted over centuries. Any visitor to Belfast now can see the force of the hostility writ large on gable walls and still burning in pallet pyres lit annually on the anniversary of significant dates. Each side is engaged in the relentless task of getting their own back, their due, their rightful portion. For each, national identity is at stake; they are claiming an idea of Ireland that belongs to them, that is rightfully theirs, and resisting the imposition of a different version of events.

What if something similar goes on for people who have suffered other impositions, other claims on what they feel is their birthright? The very idea of your self, the governing idea of the world you live in, is at stake. The fight to get your own back then carries a primitive and powerful meaning, and the energy poured into the public relations campaign needs to pack the same punch as the painted murals in Belfast.

Alvarez (2012) talks about the rightful need children express for a different sort of future, and I think the need for and right to a different sort of past is implied in her idea of the moral imperative of order, justice, and rightness. She writes that the 'paranoid position has its own logic, its own grammar and its own sanities' (Alvarez, 2012:89). One of these is the fierce knowledge that things should be and should have been different. I have written (Sutton, 2014) of a pivotal moment in a long therapy, when I was asked reproachfully, 'Where were you?' of a time long before I knew the boy asking the question. Something he felt he had a right to was missing, and the lack needed representation. If nobody is prepared to represent it – 'I' as the (m)other should have been there even though we both know in another sense I could not – the lack is insisted upon, and will need to continue to be re-presented, acted out. Alvarez's (2012) idea of 'a grammar of rightful need' is a profoundly therapeutic response to an abused child's sense of moral order, of justice, of rectification. There can be what feels like a vengeful gathering of evidence for the prosecution, and we seem to need a witness more than we need a solution. The trouble needs to continue to re-present what we are up against, until someone gets it, and makes reparation, so that we get our own back.

In fact, for most of us, getting our own back is an actual impossibility; the claim has been denied, the ground lost long ago. It is not about now. Hence the fight continues, even through the generations, because it can never be won. The best we can hope for as some kind of resolution is a recognition of loss, and a mourning of it, so that the possibilities of the actual present become available. But this involves giving up the hope of reclamation, and our innate sense of justice, among other things, keeps the flame alight.

This seems to shine a different light on the psychoanalytic concept of resistance. In connection with the neurobiology we will come to shortly, it would begin to make sense of the need to cling to troubling symptoms, not seeming to take advantage of help offered. It might offer an explanation for the seemingly puzzling business of someone spending so much time focusing on the rear-view mirror, while apparently in life's driving seat. I will think further in this chapter about how and why we try to get our own back or die in the attempt, looking at the call of the past and at developmental factors that prevent forward movement. I will discuss the neurobiology that sheds new light on the nature of resistance to treatment, and try to show how the protections that are useful in a dangerous world prevent change and development. Even in the calm, someone can be preparing themselves for the storm that experience has taught them is on its way. Such protections can be understood as necessary adaptations to adversity, but they mean that help offered is not experienced in the way helpers expect – especially as helpers may themselves be working to a script in which they have to be experienced as helpful. We will see how the re-presentation of relational reality, experienced as happening now, can thus prevent connection, and contact with what looks like reality from one or other point of view.

Reluctance to be taken in (Sutton, 2014) may be seen as resistance to treatment, and risks being understood – if symptoms are framed as belonging to the individual – as a choice, at some level, of a refusal to change. In what follows, I will consider some of the perspectives from which this standoff can be seen. First, there is the question of the disturbance of change, and of how to maintain the equilibrium of a family or national system, especially under a ministry of fear. Second, there is the cover-up, involving the vexed question of knowing while needing not to know, and needing someone else to both know and not know. Third, we will consider the wiring in of relational possibilities in these circumstances, what we might call the neurobiology of denial, along with a look at how resistance relates to loyalty and identity and the story of our life that we would lose our life to protect.

The disturbance of change

Underlying or overriding every other factor in resistance may be the need to maintain the kind of equilibrium that Joseph (1989) has written about, and that Freud may have had in mind in the 'constancy principle' (1895) which he saw as behind and beyond the pleasure principle (Freud, 1920:277). A modern way of investigating the same truth may be today's development research focus on emotional regulation. Infancy research (Beebe & Lachmann, 2002) shows the mutuality of this process: regulation is relational, not individual. Joseph's (1989) work explores the nature of psychic equilibrium, and although clinically she does not explicitly address the question of the historical derivation of symptoms, she attends minutely to the expression of them in the transference. Her microanalysis discovers her patient's history and unconscious phantasy in the to and fro of the present relationship in the session, carefully following shifts in behaviour, feeling, and atmosphere. In terms of the neurobiology of mind, the process of close attention to emotional nuance and resonance in the moment itself wires in a capacity to attend to states of mind. This relationship provides a triangulation, even a constellation, of perspectives which in itself can be regulating. Once internalized, it offers a means of self-regulation.

Freud's foundational insight linking life stories to symptoms in hysteria, a relationship that in 1895 he was still seeking in vain 'in the biographies of other psychoses' (1895:165), is predicated on the curative value of truth. He sees symptoms as communicative of that which has been deleted from the narrative, the patient acting out that which has been forgotten and repressed (1914). His technique works on the basis that uncovering the forbidden truth alleviates the symptom. Where an early patient was resistant, he is firm about the terms of engagement:

> she perhaps thought what had occurred to her was not the right thing. But that was not her business; it was her duty to remain wholly objective and to say what had come to mind, whether it was suitable or not.
>
> (Freud, 1895:158)

Schimmel (2013:48) notes that 'the reader is left with the impression that the potential psychic pain associated with recall does not seem to have been fully grasped or considered by Freud'. Despite some sudden endings, Freud does not necessarily focus in some of his case histories on the potentially dysregulating emotional impact of this technique upon his patient, even when one was 'furious with him for having betrayed her secret' to her mother (Breuer & Freud, 1895:164). He sees the talking, the bringing to mind in words, and not the responsive reflective attention, as the curative factor. His focus on the whole is on explicit content, not implicit process, like an archaeologist digging for a find. The intrinsic power imbalance reflected in this distribution of agency brings another perspective on the nature and purpose of resistance, which can be an important way of organizing against invasion and colonization. Like a colonizing power mining for minerals, the therapeutic relationship is extractive in this understanding of it. The assumption is that the clinician has a right to dig down and discover finds in the service of a cure; the patient must submit. He or she, often she in the early days of hysteria treatment, has no business considering what to bring up.

Furthermore, in classical psychoanalysis, the still face so disturbing for babies even momentarily (Tronick et al., 1975) is reflected in the analyst's famous stance of neutrality. The patient must undergo the disturbance of change without a partner in emotional regulation. The stories we will turn to shortly show the impossibility of this task, especially for children, still dependent upon the family system and unable to survive isolation.

First though, it is worth a look at the neuroscience of relating, which has implications for therapeutic technique. It has become clear, for example, that the right hemisphere is linked to implicit information processing, as opposed to the more explicit conscious processing of the left hemisphere (Happaney et al., 2004). The very way in which experience is processed is handled by the right brain, with its relational focus. The right brain is established as the core of the implicit self: 'Indeed the implicit functions and structures of the right brain represent the inner world described by psychoanalysis since its inception' (Schore, 2010:179). We take in our ways of being then, our implicit self, our unspoken sense of identity, through the feeling of what happens in relationship, rather than its content. This has important implications for clinical practice, building on Joseph's (1989) focus on implicit rather than explicit process, which Alvarez (2012) has pioneered in child psychoanalysis, and which I will go on to consider more fully in the final chapter.

Returning to Freud and the idea of resistance, I would just like to mention here that although he is interested in the idea of currency as a metaphor for psychic activity, he does not appear to consider the value of this currency as necessarily consisting in the relationship itself. He suggests, for example, that an economic motive for children's play consists in 'the yield of pleasure involved' (1920:283). The discussion that follows offers mastery and revenge as two possible yields of pleasure. Freud's idea of the child acting upon the world driven by the aim of producing these particular results suggests to me an early failure of mutual delight. The babies filmed in Beebe's (1982) study actively seek their mothers' eyes and minds for the vitality of connection itself, rather than for some secondary gain.

Furthermore, qualities of emotionality are between them, rather than in one partner or the other. Emotional regulation is a property of the dyad here – or rather the family, the felt experience of which is included in the emotional system, whether the members are present or not on any one occasion. Mutual emotional regulation maintains equilibrium and is gradually internalized, building capacity for reflecting on experience; it happens in and through qualities of relationship.

We have seen in previous chapters that in reframing a symptom as belonging to a system and not merely to the individual, the role of the symptom becomes clearer. It maintains equilibrium in the face of disturbance for which no relational regulation may be available. It may in fact feel to the symptom's carrier like vital protection of a family system against catastrophic change. In the chapter, 'It's not you, it's me: Oedipus was framed', we looked at the life stories of Kezia and Leon, who seemed to be charged with carrying a heavy intergenerational load. In those and in Jacob's story, to which I will turn shortly, disrupting the status quo felt literally unthinkable. In this sense, we can see how essential it is for the symptom to be maintained.

Bion (1970:197) has written of change which 'outrages the moral system'. Moralizing is one form of regulation; locating badness outside makes stability inside seem more achievable. This is the basis of the psychoanalytic concept of projection, which is actively used by powerful forces not only in families but by those in a society seeking to maintain a social system that works to their advantage. At the time of writing, threats of more and more 'bad' immigrants arriving into Western nations are blazed on banner headlines in UK and US newspapers. Baldwin's (1965) insight that segregation arose when white America needed a scapegoat to carry the badness of its own monstrous use of slavery is pertinent here. We project badness outside, in a 'them and us' polarity, in order to preserve the idea of goodness inside, which itself works to maintain equilibrium. We get rid of disturbance felt to come from outside, and feel justified. We get our own back on those felt to have inflicted it on us. Perhaps Freud's mastery and revenge are what we turn to on every social level in the absence of relational regulation, especially when the world feels unsafe.

When there is something traumatic, frightening, and hidden in the family, the child feels fear, but is unable to name it, or find comfort. What is ministered, distributed through care, is fear. This has a compound relational effect.

> Infants are directly affected by the traumatic event, and their symptomatology is exacerbated by the indirect effect of their caregiver's compromised responsiveness to them, which is in part a result of the caregiver's own posttraumatic symptomatology.
>
> (Scheeringa & Zeanah, 2001:809)

The child's sense of safety and attachment to her parents is compromised. If reflective function is also compromised, and it is hard for parents to feel with the child in a compassionate way because they are preoccupied with their own difficult feelings, she is left with the dysregulation fear entails, without a way of resolving it, and feels shame and humiliation. I mentioned earlier, in the section 'Seeing, being and identity', the link between the lack of a compassionate witness and shame (Schimmenti, 2012). Shame is essentially a relational experience, and the cycle of rupture and repair is a key factor in regulating it (Schore, 1998). If relational repair cannot happen, dysregulation leads to unpredictable outbursts, exacerbating feelings of shaming exposure. These are grounded in fear of rejection or humiliation in the eyes of a critical other. This fear is itself grounded in an experience of rejection or humiliation, which has been internalized into a template for relating, Bowlby's (1969) internal working model or Stern's (1998) ways-of-being-with, wired in through associations and connections made in formative early relationships.

The humiliation seems partly to be about being found wanting. By the logic of neurobiological process, this reflects the nature of the original response to the wanting, which could potentially lead to comfort or humiliation. Schore's work (1998) links meaning-making and regulation with shame. If in the meaning-making of a particular family system a child's need is disparaged and dismissed, a cover-up for vulnerability becomes necessary to avoid shaming exposure. A need that in another context is seen as natural, that finds an empathic response, has to be disavowed, even despised. This sets in motion two concurrent streams of feeling, that of resentment (re-feeling the bitterness, the injustice of it) and a wish for revenge or rectification, for getting your own back. Something essential, something one had a right to, has been taken, or withheld. Because we can never step in the same river twice, in practice we can never get it back. But we can die trying. In order to maintain the hope of finding it, we preserve the relationship that withheld it by idealizing it, and projecting our fury and disappointment onto someone else. Perhaps the almost universal hatred of stepmothers serves this need, offering a way of protecting a relationship with the mother which may not be felt to be able to withstand hostility. The two impulses of love and hate must be kept apart, in the interests of avoiding a disturbing conflict, preserving equilibrium and the hope of getting not just in the present or future, but retrospectively too, what should have been rightfully ours.

Under the surface stuckness of what psychoanalysts call resistance, then, there is internal turmoil. There are powerful crosscurrents around love and hate, and furthermore around getting to know and refusing to know. Paradoxically, in order for there to be a chance of someone being the kind of person who might want to get to know the whole story, fear, shame, hatred, resentment, and reproach have to be kept at bay, and so nobody can know the whole truth. A stand-off is inevitable, even while approach is desperately needed.

The cover-up

The dilemma of resistance then, is that I need you to know, and I need you not to know. I will turn now to Jacob's story, in which these paradoxical impulses played out. I will consider the conflicting relational truths they expressed, along with some of the urgent reasons people had for clinging to the cover-up that prevents connection.

Jacob was fourteen when he was referred to a child and adolescent mental health clinic because he wanted to die. He had recently discovered by accident at a family gathering that he been adopted by his grandmother, as his mother had died during his birth. There was no mention of his birth father. The referral mentioned the 'mixed feelings' his grand/mother had about Jacob, which seemed like a light term bearing a heavy load.

The impression Jacob made was of someone physically fragile and mentally alert. He had an air of obliviousness, although on close observation he seemed to be highly vigilant. It was as if he needed to notice, but not be noticed noticing. At the clinic, there was a good natured, light touch feeling about the first few meetings with the family which made it surprisingly hard to register the import of the referral. This scenario at once revealed and hid the nature of the problem. The fact that Jacob was actually reeling from shock and loss, to the extent of not wanting to live, was obscured. This double take, the disparity between content and presentation, was instructive.

For adopted children, as for anyone with a traumatic relational history, there are inherent difficulties in knowing and living with the truth of their circumstances. These difficulties can prevent them making the truth an integrated part of their story, their sense of themselves. Very often, those around them and they themselves at times seem to rely on applying Freud's 'patch over the place where originally a rent had appeared' (1924:151) in their relationship with the outside world. They turn Steiner's (1993) blind eye towards what cannot be borne. These protections are necessary when there has been a catastrophe that threatens the survival of our sense of ourselves. Jacob had experienced such a catastrophe, not only in the news of his adoption, but in the unspoken emotional charge of it over his lifetime. Simmonds writes:

> Adoption and the adopted child may … generally be regarded as symptomatic of things that are embedded in the family history but which cannot be thought or talked about … knowledge and curiosity about it are thought to be better avoided because of the dangerous story they may tell.
>
> (Simmonds, 2008:31)

Jacob was surprisingly open to begin with about the dangerous story, but it soon became clear that this truth was agonizing for all concerned. It necessitated a protective cover-up which looked a lot like resistance, for knowledge and curiosity were avoided to shut out an outside perspective and protect internal and relational fragility.

In one of his earliest sessions, Jacob muttered to his therapist, like it was a guilty secret, 'My parents are other people'. By this double-edged phrase, he meant both that his parents as he had known them had turned out to be other people, and also that other people – people he had never met – were his birth parents. He talked urgently about the impact of this on all his family relationships: his siblings were in fact his aunts and uncles. The sense of shock and betrayal was palpable. Perhaps the most striking thing of all was that it still felt like forbidden knowledge. Even though he knew, and now his therapist did, too, it was as if it was not supposed to be known. There was a need for a cover-up. Like the cheerful early meetings with the family, in which the story was told but its emotional import was deleted, there was a disconnect.

He told this secret after seeing a documentary on Egyptian pyramids, and mummification, which showed ancient mummies wrapped in layers of bindings, lying deep below ground. He conveyed a sense of tip-toeing around the terrifying possibility that if the site were to be excavated, he would fall through the cover-up into the dead place himself. He could convey the dangerous truth to his therapist, as a kind of secret ally, but then they were both at risk, and would have to keep well clear of the danger area. He seemed to feel both longing and dread; he both wanted and feared to find the dead mother and a place to belong. It was as if in doing so he would lose contact with the world of life, because the representation in his mind of someone like the therapist would not maintain the connection while Jacob searched. It became apparent that he himself maintained the connection with the (m)other person through constant monitoring of their emotional state. If he stopped, the link between them would be dropped and he would be lost. In an effort to distract himself and divert his therapist from exploring/initiating this terrifying possibility, he drew himself up and engaged her in a rather manic smiley way. It left her with a dilemma: Jacob did need her to know about these very painful frightening things, but he was terrified of anyone noticing them, in case it severed the connection. The double take of the family meeting remained – there were feelings to be taken in at gut level, but also a desperate need for the surface to remain undisturbed. The idea that anyone could take in his disturbing feelings and maintain the connection with him, rather than themselves be disturbed and cut him off, seemed impossible for Jacob. I think he felt the link with his family was broken, possibly irreparably. Indeed, the world as he knew it was broken. He was lost in a dark dead space if he did not pour his energies into maintaining an earlier state of things, preventing the disturbance of the tragedy that had already happened.

According to the mutual regulation model (Gianino & Tronick, 1988), for any baby, the caregiver is a crucial part of the development of their capacity for responsive reflection, which helps them apprehend and process emotion. Given the circumstances of Jacob's birth, this was made all the more necessary and all the more difficult for his grand/mother to do. Jacob was evidence of her daughter's death, and felt at some level to be the cause of it. What is more, he looked very like her. The force of all this on his grand/mother's emotional equilibrium was enormous. It inevitably diminished her availability to Jacob as a partner in emotional regulation, curious about his feeling state and willing to be open to emotional connection. The difficulties his very presence evoked for her constituted relational stress for the infant Jacob. So the primary maternal preoccupation that Winnicott describes (1956), or Bion's maternal reverie (1962), laying a foundation for the baby's sense of self, was compromised. Jacob found himself at fourteen trying to face a terrible shock that shook him to the core, with reduced capacity in his parents' minds to help him, because of the extraordinary and enduring pain of their circumstances. Reading the ensuing protections as resistance would seem rather callous. As Alvarez (2018) puts it, 'Truth can be contained in the so-called defence'. Bion writes of lies as 'formulations known by the initiator to be false but maintained as a barrier against statements that lead to a psychological upheaval' (1970:97). There are things we cannot let ourselves know. The upheaval against which the lie is mobilized is one of catastrophic change that has already happened, a change that threatens the person's experience of and valuation of himself, outraging his moral system.

The disparity between the family's cheerful presentation and the severity of Jacob's fear of catastrophic upheaval was represented in a dream he had in which his brother/uncle hurtled down the road towards him, laughing in a fairground dodgem car. A crash was imminent, in which he would be killed, and he woke up terrified. The turning of the threat to his life into a fairground car was telling. Jacob developed the protection of a kind of comedy act, in which worrying things were turned into cartoonish fun and games. This was his way of finding some expression for his fears in a way that would not destabilize his family system. The nature of this family system as he experienced it was reflected in a second dream involving a song and dance routine he was forced to maintain, under threat of death from two 'friendly' people with a gun to his head. Not noticing, and maintaining a jolly cover-up, was evidently deadly serious. There was a feeling of something very cruel. The connection seemed to be severed between feeling life-threatening danger and being able to notice and respond to it in a compassionate way.

Joseph (1982) has written powerfully about near death experience, describing a distorted and self-destructive response to life-threatening danger. On the evidence of the neurobiology, this response seems not so much internal as internalized, a way of being that has been wired in through a formative primary relationship. It is not intrinsic to Jacob himself, or did not begin that way, but rather grew out of the relations between the people in his life story, including himself, and their tragic circumstances (Balbernie, 2001). It is then reinforced by relational experience, in the anticipation machine of the mind (Siegel, 1999).

In a family world where other concerns prevail over truth and meaning-seeking, we wire in ways of surviving in that world of relating. If the going-on-being of the family means that certain relational truths cannot be discovered, its members, particularly its smallest, weakest members, must live by that creed. If power-seeking prevails, there is a continuing assumption of cruelty, of being sequestered or exploited for others' use, wired in through original experience. The feeling of not being attended to, of your needs being problematic, is confirmed by later perception of experience. In this case, it can of course be an assumption to which some excitement is harnessed; if you get your retaliation in first, at least it carries a glow of power. Perhaps a power-based connection might even mean excitement and glory, in the absence of the hope of a more attuned and emotionally resonant connection. The unwelcome alternative may be to be found wanting, with all the shame that carries when your needs cannot be met.

The relational roots of denial

We have seen that neuroscience has confirmed the experience-dependent nature of mind development. I do not know where that leaves Klein's (1957) constitutional envy, but it seems to me that we have to take the relational building of mind into account in thinking about death drive and envy just as much as we do in more benign manifestations of experience-dependent emotion and attitude.

The question of whether we are turning a blind eye to the death drive seems apposite. Clinical experience along with neurobiology suggests that if, in our earliest relationships, problematic aspects of our experience cannot be seen or taken in by the other and Steiner's (1993) blind eye is turned, they are experienced as unseeable, untakeinable – essentially incompatible with connection. This dynamic leads to a shaming isolation, in which paradoxically the only possible connection is at the expense of authentic self-experience. This means self-sabotage is inevitable, one way or the other – either through desperately driven inauthentic performance, like Jacob's song and dance routine with a gun to his head, or by the direct self-harm expressed in his suicidality. It becomes apparent to someone in Jacob's position that his own presence in the family is the cause of the trouble, and so getting rid of himself comes into view as a way of resolving the problem.

Suicidality, along with what has been called the death instinct, thus has relational roots; it does not belong to the individual but to their relational experience. It is deadly and deadening, but it is a response to deadly and deadening experience. Adam's long slow suicide attempt is a case in point. It exemplifies an idea of resistance, for he certainly clung to his anorexic symptoms for years, in one treatment after another. He seemed, in one way of framing his clinical presentation, to be utterly resistant to the prospect of getting better, to be triumphing over, even trashing his therapists in their inability to connect with him and make sense of their relationship. However, I think getting to know a bit more about the neuroscience of this dynamic helps us frame it differently.

One of the effects of trauma on the brain is that neuronal pathways are intensively created in parts of the brain that stimulate hypervigilance. It makes evolutionary sense that the brain develops adaptively in relation to the situation in which the baby finds himself. A hard-wired 'superhighway' develops in adversity, through which new experience is filtered. This is useful in a dangerous world, as was Adam's in his early years. However, it also means the parts of Adam's brain that process ordinary positive experience wither; they are not so vital for survival. His prefrontal cortex, hippocampus, and connecting corpus callosum are shrunk, and his amygdala is more reactive. His supercharged sympathetic nervous system is on red alert, increasing blood pressure, adrenaline level, and heart rate to levels that often go beyond fright or flight, requiring the body's collapse into a freeze response of helpless hopelessness. These responses are not balanced by a parasympathetic system that would bring his body down into a relaxed and calmer state of being, allowing him to connect warmly with other people, so that his body begins to produce oxytocin, the best antidote for human stress.

This physiological adaptation may present in the clinic as resistance to treatment, and risks being understood – if symptoms are framed as belonging to the individual – as a choice, at some level, of a desire not to connect and get to know, Bion's (1959) –K link. Another way of seeing it though, is as a psychophysiological system adapted to the world in which someone finds himself, where connections are dangerous, and the disturbing risks of getting to know are too great.

Jacob's family story is an example of how Bion's (1959) K and -K, getting to know and refusing to know, reflect qualities of formative relationships that have been internalized early in life. Bion writes of how,

> In some prepsychotic states the individual has an "internal object" which hates emotion, especially because emotion links the individual to reality and external objects (both of which constitute threats to the narcissistic trends of the disturbed person)
> (1959:308)

I think we need to consider the derivation of the disturbance in the disturbed person he mentions, and begin to think of internalized, and not just internal, objects. What if the reality to which the emotional response is linked is unthinkable in the family world? It seems clear that if our experience is of a world in which meaning has to be disavowed, emotions stop making sense, and have to be disavowed too. The need to be divorced from reality is enough to make anyone psychotic. No wonder the individual he has in mind hates emotion, and its link with reality; for Jacob as he grew up, neither the emotion nor the reality from which it arose could be seen to exist.

Disturbance is not a quality intrinsic to the personality, it is a quality of relational experience, wired in through dysregulating relationship. Denial, too, or the quality that Bion calls -K, is characteristic not of an individual per se, but of a family system, a world in which it is not safe to get to know, to explore. In Adam's violent early world, for example, there was no room for curiosity; all resources were directed towards self-preservation and the maintenance of a fragile equilibrium. The cover-up of resistance expresses a relational truth: this is happening and no one wants to know about it. Furthermore, I cannot risk them knowing about it, because that would destroy the relationship in which that might one day be possible.

Holding this disturbing conflict is exhausting, and a precarious equilibrium can only be maintained at the cost of a lively open connection with others. It is therefore experienced as deadly. Psychoanalytic thinkers over the years have thought about the death instinct as an impulse to shut down and close off life and connection. Freud links it to 'a need to restore an earlier state of things' (1920:331). But what if the primary connection was experienced as deadening? What if in an earlier state of things nobody was available to be delighted by the baby, to play and to get to know him? How would that be conveyed from one body and mind to another, other than through a deadening of relational connection? It does not make sense to think of a baby seeking a deadening connection from the womb, but it makes neurobiological sense to think of a tiny child with an overwhelmed or preoccupied mother desperately needing a lively connection, partly despairing of ever getting it and partly trying to shut down and make as few demands as possible to protect the fragile connection he has. Given the brain and nervous system's function as an anticipation machine, expecting the earlier state of things to prevail, this shutdown to avoid the shame of being found wanting is likely to be reinforced, especially if adversity continues. Thus the past has the power to close down potentiality and new connections. The development research we have seen shows how these and other relational truths find expression through the body. Deadening relational truths can thus be conveyed to a sensitive other, provided they are not already occupied by their own distress, and livelier connections sought and found through the qualities of the new relationship, as Alvarez's work (1992, 2004, 2012) abundantly shows.

The neurobiology I have mentioned briefly above underlines the need for our idea of reality to encompass the neurobiological import of transference. The relational truth that Jacob or Adam re-present is their actual experience of the world in the present moment, the relational past in the present relationship. This holds whether the experienced relational truth is benign or malign. Bion's sense that 'healthy mental growth seems to depend on truth' (Bion, 1965:38) applies just as much to communicating the absence of a responsive (m)other as it does her presence. The dilemma about what can be known is itself a representation of relational truth, an unearthed clue, in archaeological terms. For example, the drawing one day of a grotesquely greedy boy gave a clue to the kind of trap Adam might be in, hiding in Steiner's (1993) psychic retreat from two disturbing possibilities. The first was a worry about an all-consuming hunger emerging which he experienced as grotesque and repellent – being found wanting everything. The second was a confusing reluctance to have anyone attend to his need, because it might make him feel better, and then no one would need to attend to him, and so everyone would go away. He needed to be hungry, to keep his mother near. The symptom preserved a stasis with which he could live, however precariously. The symptom is protective, in the way that a protection racket is protective.

Furthermore, in embodying his suicidal father, there seemed to be a fierce loyalty not only to him, but to the missing vulnerable little boy he had once been, who bore the impact of that traumatic event without the availability of a mediating mind to witness his experience. He needed to deny the help on offer, to show how at the crucial moment, nobody was there to help. As for Aisha's mother, help was experienced as unhelpful disconfirmation of the relational truth he was trying to communicate. I think Adam's and Jacob's stories shine a light on the dilemma of resistance, and both suggest a clinical way forward that pays as much attention to the implicit relational qualities of the therapeutic relationship as to the explicit content of sessions. Who am I for you? is a clinical question always worth holding in mind, along with, Who do you think you are for me? and of course, the therapist's own question, Who are you for me?

The role of language as the means by which the import of relational experience is conveyed, contained, understood and returned is worth thinking about here. Even when we are witnessed, and someone tries to name our experience, of absence or disconnection, for example, we run into the difficulty of the gap between experience and language, Bion's (1970) illusion of naming. The words can never capture the whole experience, and there is potential for any amount of distortion in the account we give (Panksepp & Solms, 2012). Disparity arises between the truth of an experience and how it is described. This gap is a place for comedy when it is not too wide; it can be a place for oppression, and for what we understand as madness, when the gap cannot be breached.

Alvarez (1997) has called for a better understanding of the grammar of projective identification as communication once this madness-inducing breach between experience and narrative has happened. She suggests that therapeutic understandings then need to prioritize rightful developmental needs rather than what can be seen as omnipotent wishes. She distinguishes between defences and overcomings in the paranoid position. Alongside rectification fantasies of vengeance, she elucidates rectification fantasies of justice and other moral imperatives; both are ways of getting your own back, but the second feels developmentally more hopeful. Her distinction underlines the significance of examining the countertransference (Joseph, 1989) with all the honesty and delicate sensitivity the therapist can muster as potential emotional information about the patient's state of mind. For Jacob to relinquish the protection of his comedy act, with its assumed obliviousness to feeling, or Adam his self-starvation, his denial of need, they would each have to feel that somebody really got the turmoil beneath the denial. They need someone who can take the disturbance, the hate and the reproach, can even take in and understand the desire not to know or be known, and yet still keep the connection alive. I will go on to consider the nature of the responsibility this entails in the final chapter.

References

Alvarez, A. (1992). *Live Company: Psychoanalytic Psychotherapy with Autistic, Borderline, Deprived and Abused Children*. London: Routledge.

Alvarez, A. (1997). Projective identification as a communication: Its grammar in borderline psychotic children. *Psychoanalytic Dialogues*, 7(6):753–768.

Alvarez, A. (2004). Finding the wavelength: Tools in communication in children with autism. *Journal of Infant Observation*, 7(2):91–106.

Alvarez, A. (2012). *The Thinking Heart: Three Levels of Psychoanalytic Therapy with Disturbed Children*. London: Routledge.

Alvarez, A. (2018). *Future Perfect: Some reflections on the sense of anticipation in ordinary infants and in psychoanalytic work*. Paper presented at New Zealand Association of Psychotherapists Conference 2018. Retrieved from www.youtube.com/watch?v=jCFXvbc-jk8.

Balbernie, R. (2001). Circuits and circumstances: The neurobiological consequences of early relationship experiences and how they shape later behaviour. *Journal of Child Psychotherapy*, 27(3):237–255.

Baldwin, J. (1965). *Cambridge Debate: Has the American Dream Been Achieved at the Expense of the American Negro?* Retrieved from www.youtube.com/watch?v=nbkObXxSUus.

Beebe, B. (1982). Micro-timing in mother-infant communication. In M. R. Key (ed.), *Nonverbal Communication Today,* Vol. 33:169–195. New York: Mouton.

Beebe, B. & Lachmann, F. (2002). *Infant Research and Adult Treatment: Co-constructing Interactions*. London: Analytic.

Bion, W. R. (1959). Attacks on linking. *International Journal of Psychoanalysis*, 40:308–315.

Bion, W. R. (1962). *Learning from Experience*. London: Heinemann.

Bion, W.R. (1965). *Transformations*. London: Heinemann.

Bion, W.R. (1970). *Attention and Interpretation*. New York: Basic.

Bowlby, J. (1969). *Attachment and Loss, 1*. New York: Basic.

Breuer, J. & Freud, S. (1895). Studies in hysteria. In J. Strachey (Ed. & Trans.), *The Standard Edition of the Complete Psychological Works of Sigmund Freud*, Vol. 2:1–335. London: Hogarth.

Freud, S. (1914). Remembering, repeating and working-through. In J. Strachey (Ed. & Trans.), *The Standard Edition of the Complete Psychological Works of Sigmund Freud*, Vol. 12:147–156. London: Hogarth.

Freud, S. (1920). Beyond the pleasure principle. In J. Strachey (Ed. & Trans.), *The Standard Edition of the Complete Psychological Works of Sigmund Freud*, Vol. 18:7–64. London: Hogarth.

Freud, S. (1924). Neurosis and psychosis. In J. Strachey (Ed. & Trans.), *The Standard Edition of the Complete Psychological Works of Sigmund Freud,* Vol. 19:147–153. London: Hogarth.

Freud, S. (1950). Project for a Scientific Psychology (1950 [1895]). *The Standard Edition of the Complete Psychological Works of Sigmund Freud,* Vol I (1886–1899): Pre-Psycho-Analytic Publications and Unpublished Drafts, 281–391.

Gianino, A., & Tronick, E. Z. (1988). The mutual regulation model: The infant's self and interactive regulation and coping and defensive capacities. In T. M. Field, P. M. McCabe, & N. Schneiderman (Eds.), *Stress and Coping across Development*:47–68. Hillsdale, NJ: Lawrence Erlbaum.

Happaney, K., Zelazo, P. D., & Stuss, D. T. (2004). Development of orbitofrontal function: Current themes and future directions. *Brain and Cognition*, 55:1–10.

Joseph, B. (1982). Addiction to near-death. *International Journal Psychoanalysis*, 63(4):449–456.

Joseph, B. (1989). New library of psychoanalysis, 9. In M. Feldman and E. Bott Spillius (Eds.), *Psychic Equilibrium and Psychic Change: Selected Papers of Betty Joseph*. London: Tavistock.

Klein, M. (1957). Envy and gratitude. In B. Joseph, E. O'Shaughnessy & H. Segal (Eds.) *Envy and Gratitude & Other Works, 1946–1963*. Hogarth: London, 176–246.

Panksepp, J. & Solms, M. (2012). What is neuropsychoanalysis? Clinically relevant studies of the minded brain. *Trends in Cognitive Sciences*, 16(1):6–8.

Scheeringa, M. S. & Zeanah, C. H. (2001). A relational perspective on PTSD in early childhood. *Journal of Traumatic Stress*, 14(4):799–815.

Schimmel, P. (2013). *Sigmund Freud's Discovery of Psychoanalysis: Conquistador and Thinker*. London: Routledge.

Schimmenti, A. (2012). Unveiling the hidden self: Developmental trauma and pathological shame. *Psychodynamic Practice: Individuals, Groups & Organizations*, 18(2):195–211.

Schore, A. N. (1998). Early shame experiences & the development of the infant brain. In Gilbert, P. & Andrews, B. (Eds.), *Shame: Interpersonal Behaviour, Psychopathology & Culture*. London: Oxford University, 57–77.

Schore, A. N. (2010). The right brain implicit self: A central mechanism of the psychotherapy change process. In J. Petrucelli (Ed.), *Knowing, Not-knowing and Sort of Knowing: Psychoanalysis and the Experience of Uncertainty*:177–202. London: Karnac.

Siegel, D. J. (1999). *The Developing Mind: Toward a Neurobiology of Interpersonal Experience*. New York: Guilford.

Simmonds, J. (2008). Developing a curiosity about adoption: A psychoanalytic perspective. In D. Hindle & G. Shulman (Eds.), *The Emotional Experience of Adoption*:27–41. London: Routledge.

Steiner, J. (1993). *Psychic Retreats: Pathological Organisations in Psychotic, Neurotic and Borderline Patients*. London: Routledge.

Stern, D. (1998). The process of therapeutic change involving implicit knowledge: Some implications of developmental observations for adult psychotherapy. *Infant Mental Health Journal*, 19:300–308.

Sutton, S. (2014). *Being Taken In: The Framing Relationship*. London: Karnac.

Tronick, E., Adamson, L.B., Als, H., & Brazelton, T.B. (1975). *Infant emotions in normal and pertubated interactions*. Presentation at the biennial meeting of the Society for Research in Child Development, Denver, CO.

Winnicott, D. W. (1956). Primary maternal preoccupation. In D. W. Winnicott *Collected Papers, through Paediatrics to Psychoanalysis*:300–305. London: Tavistock.

Chapter 6

It's not rocket science, it's neuroscience

It has become crystal clear that the impact of trauma, especially on children as their minds and bodies develop, is a major public health concern. Children subjected to toxic stress – repeated, extreme activation of their stress response – during critical periods of development, suffer lifelong consequences. The Adverse Childhood Experiences (ACEs) study (Felitti et al., 1998) is a huge set of longitudinal data from the US, beginning in the 1990s, linking ACEs with lifelong negative effects on a person's well-being. They are cumulatively associated with significant increases in all kinds of negative social, emotional, mental, and physical health outcomes. Children with four or more ACEs are four times more likely to suffer from depression, eight times more likely to become alcoholics, and twenty times more likely to use intravenous drugs. Toxic stress affects their developing brain, immune system, cardiovascular system, and metabolic regulatory system. In fact, it is not just humans who suffer in this prolonged way from early relational damage; other primates, too, subjected to early neglect and deprivation continue to be hyperaroused by triggers linked to the trauma, and to react to these as to a return of the trauma itself. They tend to engage in violent relationships, to be hyperaggressive, or fail to protect themselves and their offspring (van der Kolk, 1989).

The idea that any of these well-identified species-wide post-traumatic symptoms can be treated as an individual characteristic when they are an adaptation to threat, and to being insufficiently buffered against adversity, seems misguided and even cruel. A degree of plasticity continues throughout life, but for good or ill, brain patterns that guide development are mostly set at moments of sensitivity during the earliest months and years (Perry, 2001a). In fact, the very earliest days are the most formative of all (Perry et al., 2018); it is harder to recover from relational adversity in the first two months than it is to recover from adversity for many years thereafter, if the first two months were kind to us.

It is time to take what we now know about the relational, experience-dependent nature of our psychobiological development into account clinically. An intergenerational trauma history is vital for our understanding of what children and the adults they grow into have been through, that is still going through their bodies and minds. Yet trauma histories are often not recognized in clinical practice. Mauritz et al. (2013), reviewing 30 years of psychiatric cases and 33 studies, found that people with severe mental illness have significantly higher levels of interpersonal trauma than the general population, and yet abuse and neglect, complex PTSD, and dissociative disorders are scarcely examined. This is odd: there is a clearly established link between trauma and mental illness, and yet it is not necessarily seen as clinically relevant.

In working over many years in child and adolescent mental health, in education and in fostering and adoption, I have noticed that it can be extraordinarily hard in some organizational cultures, despite the evidence, to see how we are each of us affected by relational experience and defined by the understanding of those in charge of the narrative. We have to ask ourselves, what are we doing when we ignore the family story embodied in mental health symptoms? Why are children seen out of the context of their relational experience, given decades of neuroscience establishing that minds are wired by and through relating? It is hard to know. Akomfrah's (1986) film *Handsworth Songs* comes to mind, which highlights the power dynamic and inherent conflict in the war of naming the problem. Who decides what is wrong? It is often those in power. In fact the ability to define the frame and the kind of language used may constitute their power, as the Black Panther group explained, fighting systemic injustice in segregated America in the 1960s. This truth, of course, is the basis of media empires.

In the smaller scale power balance of the family, or the mental health clinic, it is bewilderingly easy to label a child for behaviour problems, and even to insist on his taking responsibility for his actions. It is much more difficult to hear the message his behaviour communicates about his expectation of relationships, especially as we now know these are wired in through early experience. Something about holding a parent responsible seems to feel frightening. Does it feel too close to an accusation of blame? If so, is this perhaps partly to do with an identification with the parents? I wonder if it may also be because even as adults, we have a wired in dependence from early days that warns against such a risky attribution. If we receive strong implicit messages as young children about what our parents can manage, it might still feel dangerous all these years later to overload them, or authority figures in their place. Are we as professionals perhaps unconsciously turning a blind eye to the failures of our own internal parents, protecting our idea of them and directing our resentment and desire to get our own back on the children we see?

Another possibility is that this blind spot relates to the pernicious and widespread idea of meritocracy, which holds that we get what we deserve. The sense that some of us are just innately better than others, and so rise to the top, is widespread; though it ignores the way in which minds are made, and life paths established. This false belief arises from the left brain's tendency to rationalize after the event. Tellingly, it is espoused by the powerful in a way that serves self-interest: because things are so much better for me than for others, it must be that I, and they, deserve our different fates. Such a belief would serve the equilibrium of the status quo, removing unsettling doubts about the claims of compassion, justice, and equality.

Whatever the reasons for this troubling oversight of the link between damaging life experience at a critical developmental moment and mental ill health, it is high time to change tack in the mental health clinic and in children's services in general. We need to recognize the import of the neuroscience and development studies and respond to symptoms as expressing relational experience and not an effort of will, or a natural endowment. We need to look at the relationships missing from the story that make sense of the symptoms, and see in disturbed behaviour the impact of trauma or failure of regulation and not a character flaw. Mental health symptoms are characteristic not of an individual but of their life experience, and are to be understood as the body's metaphor, expressing the unthinkable.

The neuroscience that shines a light on the relational roots of mental health also points the way ahead for clinical technique. Damasio (1999:40) shows how neuroscience, even cognitive neuroscience, has 'finally endorsed emotion'. Gallese (2009) explains how embodied simulation, through mirror neurons, of another's emotional state mediates our capacity to share the meaning of actions, intentions, feelings and emotions with others, providing the neurobiological basis of transference and countertransference. Schore's (2012) great work, *The Science of the Art of Psychotherapy*, links emotionality, meaning-making, regulation, and the development of mind. Our sense of identity emerges from this relational process. States of body and mind become established as identity traits (Perry et al., 1995) in relational sense-making stories of who we are. I will go on to think about how we might begin to incorporate different perspectives in our therapeutic sense-making in order to see the process of identification differently, lightening the load for children and adolescents like Aisha, Adam, Kezia, Leon, Maria, Shaun, Clare, and Jacob. Finally, in relation to this, we will consider the role of response in responsibility, and look at some of the work pointing the way forward for therapeutic change.

States, traits, and relocation

We have seen that experiences actually organize the developing brain, especially at moments of particular sensitivity. This means the brain can be structured as it develops by adaptive response patterns in the face of threat. The more trauma triggers a state of hyperarousal or dissociation as an adaptive response in a child, the more likely the child is to develop psychiatric symptoms. Acute adaptive states, when they persist, can thus become maladaptive traits. 'Children are not resilient, children are malleable' (Perry et al., 1995:285). The smaller the person, the greater the impact – what's more, fear makes the wolf look bigger. The most severe impact is when children are exposed to threat to and from what Balbernie (2013) has called a 'scaregiver'. Since the frightened or frightening carer is the source both of fear and of protection for children like Shaun, they experience irresolvable fear without solution. This results in unintegrated states of mind; dissociation is necessary to preserve the only available potentially protective relationship. Clinically, we meet adolescents like Adam who have had to disavow the need for closeness and protection itself, in order to protect themselves from the fear they experienced as little children and still anticipate. This is neurobiologically informed resistance. It is not a personal choice, it is a survival mechanism taken out of context. The symptom/adaptation persists through life, overriding efforts to connect, because our whole body system prioritizes survival.

In the chapter 'It's not you, it's me: Oedipus was framed', we saw how the prevailing dynamic of the parental world, whether predominantly safe or dangerous, with all its other qualities, is internalized and becomes the way in which the world is understood. Unresolved fears that preoccupy parents become shadow forces in the child's internal(ized) world. In such a family, a child can be used, as Kezia and Leon were, to express aspects of these shadows, troubling feelings disowned by the parents. The feelings find re-presentation in the relationship with the child, whose resulting state of mind and body becomes established in the way we have seen above. It is then recognized as a trait. It is attributed to the child as a personal characteristic, which is a way of establishing meaning and thus equilibrium in the family system. A child like Kezia tries to find some relation to what is evoked in her, and is confused and attacked in accepting the identification, and confused and isolated in rejecting it.

I have found that in the clinical consideration of this process, a blind eye is often turned to the developmental experience that has brought it about. To ignore the dependency of the child upon their parents, and conversely the power of the parents over their child, is to eliminate a vital part of the picture. We seem to be in a system that cannot afford to get to know about this, for fear of destabilization. Thus the child continues to carry the load. Describing disturbed behaviour as a child's choice, in a clinic, school, or youth justice system, exacerbates the denial of responsibility and further blames and shames the child. A state of mind, say a meltdown, is assigned as characteristic of a child like Aisha, a trait. A fictional identity is thereby created and to some degree inhabited, which consciously or unconsciously serves the parents' ends. It takes the place of an authentic sense of self arising from a more attuned response to the child's own impulse and need.

This process of identification by attribution of unthinkable feelings seems to go on at every level of human relating. As a society we do this to groups we see as not-us; the element of race, for example, is entirely fictitious biologically. In the world of psychoanalysis, this kind of attribution of feelings is called projection, or projective identification when whole aspects of identity are attributed. Psychoanalysts have tended on the whole in clinical work to focus on their use as an individual defence. What, though, if these imports and exports are an inevitable part of being in relation, of being in a family system? Symptoms are then a property not of the individual but of the formative family system in which they emerge – just as our temperature is not located in any one place in the body, but is a product of the whole body system.

Symptoms, like any other properties of a system, cannot be reduced to parts; they are produced in relationship, in-betweenness.

In understanding their meaning in the kind of stories we have thought about throughout the book, we need to consider what symptoms are telling us about relationships in the whole intergenerational family – and, importantly, the wider social system. Melzak and McClatchey (2019), for example, in writing about work with refugees, have described the significant beneficial impact for all community members when the political and social sources of their suffering are publicly acknowledged and memorialized. They stress the value of de-individualizing the traumatic loss and tremendous sense of guilt that can accompany community violence and war.

The traditional practice in child and adolescent mental health clinics, however, seems to have been to tend to focus almost exclusively on the individual. For example, there is the all too typical story of a young child brought to a mental health clinic by his mother, who worried about his violent outbursts. His assessment concluded that he met the DSM-IV criteria for generalized anxiety disorder, without anyone wondering what he might have been anxious about. He was given an impact score, which measures the extent to which a child's behaviour is felt to be a burden on the family, without anybody measuring the burden his family might be placing on him. Therapy goals were set for work which aimed not to understand why he worried or became dysregulated, not to think about what might be going on in his family world, but to increase his assertiveness and develop his self-esteem. These sound like worthy objectives, but they miss the point. Furthermore, this response confirms anxiety as an identifying characteristic of the child, rather than of his situation, past or present.

It helps separate out a child's sense of himself from his family's situation when we can reflect upon what his symptoms may tell us about what he has been through, that is still going through his mind and body. This clinical response locates the disturbance in a different place. It sees anxiety as performing its actual physiological function as a signal of something wrong – even if that something has already happened. We need to take into account the human reality that we adapt to our social context and are affected by the emotional states of those around us. Furthermore, it is clinically useful – unmaddening – in itself to see how the identification process works. The enormous potentiality that each of us contains as we arrive in the world is channelled adaptively through billions of neural connections to the particular circumstances, sense- and story-making of our unique family, social, and cultural context, with all its intergenerational inheritance.

Putting the response in responsibility

It becomes clear, then, that the very fact of a mental health symptom implies a failure of responsive connection, so that the emotion stays in the body and feels like a property of the self and not the situation. Nobody is available at the right time to receive the call and respond in a way that makes sense of the emotional communication. There is a failure of contingent responsiveness (Bornstein, 1989), which provides direct and immediate feedback on the baby's communication. Developmental research has shown just how early babies detect contingency in face-to-face interactions (Murray & Trevarthen, 1986), and how distressing they find non-contingent responses from their mother. This kind of attuned relational responsiveness feels like goodness to the developing child (Fairbairn, 1946). It establishes a sense of truth and authenticity, and when it is available, the child feels the vitality of being safe and loved in a relational world that feels essentially safe and loving. What is more, the world is experienced as being in creative dynamic relation to the child's impulse, fostering a sense of agency and worth. An authentic contingent response to the child's expression of feeling thus lays a crucial foundation for mental health, along with a sense of self in relation to others. The lack of it, where there is a distorted or an absent response, feels like badness. As we have seen, the question of what to do with this feeling of badness, where to locate it, is extremely problematic, at its worst necessitating a dissociation, a lack of contact with reality, that gets diagnosed as psychosis.

The crucial role of responsiveness in mental health is borne out by the neuroscientist Ramachandran (2012), who writes that many kinds of mental illness arise from disturbances in the equilibrium of reciprocity between self and others. When things have gone wrong, when there has been relational adversity, when stressed and preoccupied carers have not been able to offer the contingent responsiveness that feels like goodness to a developing child, the question of responsibility is, who needs to respond and how?

Clinically, the challenge is to make connections through resonance with undercurrents of felt experience, when there has been absence, dissonance or distortion. We need to respond in a way that's close enough to the music of what happens to be useful to someone like Clare, so that through an attuned relationship she can begin to get to know vital elements of her experience, and take the risk of disturbing the superficially harmonious way of relating that excludes them. The alternative is that she bears the risk, she carries the conflict and is sacrificed in service of the preservation of the family system.

I mentioned earlier the neurobiological basis for the process of resonance (Iacoboni, 2009), which links with the psychoanalytic notion of countertransference, and offers a way of getting in touch with these excluded elements of experience. Non-verbal signals through gaze, facial expression and gestures convey information to a responsive other, body to body. When we face each other, emotion is actually conveyed, and physiological changes occur in response: heart rates can rise, stomachs churn, breathing is affected. We can see from this how crucial face-to-face contact is in therapeutic engagement, and how much reparative connection is missed through the protection (for the therapist) of the couch in classical psychoanalysis. In a parallel with the mother and baby relationship, shifts in our inner bodily states can be reflected upon by the therapist's right prefrontal cortex. This process offers a way of connecting with the implicit (Schore, 2010), the untold story, so that it can gradually become part of a new unfolding story of what happens between people.

In re-establishing connection, or the hope of connection, implicit disturbing elements of past relational experience will inevitably impact on the here and now of the therapeutic relationship. The disturbing experience of re-presentation can be mystifying without an understanding of the process of transference. Klein's neurobiologically valid suggestion is that 'total situations' springing from 'the earliest experiences, situations and emotions' (Klein, 1952:14) are transferred from the past into the present.

What is sometimes seen in her thinking and that of her followers as the baby's innate hostility (Rosenfeld, 1964), however, is not borne out by the development research. This shows babies trying to connect with every capacity they can muster, and enjoying a lively connection with their parents when that is available. Now that we have the development research to draw on, we can see just how formative is the role of the parental response, contingent, or otherwise, in understanding the baby's expression. The baby's emotional experience in the relationship with their caregiver establishes psychobiological patterns that regulate the growth and organization of the developing brain (Schore, 1996). To present an idea of the baby as intrinsically hostile in ways that are unrelated to these early establishing patterns of interrelation seems invalid in the light of the infancy research and clinically unhelpful. When this relationship goes well, the two minds tune in and out, reattuning when there has been a rupture, in a way that enhances positive and minimizes negative emotionality. When it does not go so well, we can plainly see how ghosts in the parents' nursery (Fraiberg et al., 1975) preoccupy their minds and get in the way, preventing a clear response to the baby's impulse.

Either way, these patterns are wired into the processing function of the baby's brain. If a parent, who becomes represented in the baby's mind through Schore's psychobiological patterns, has not been able to respond in a way that repairs relational rupture, how can the child under the sway of such internalized patterns of relating be able to do it differently? They are stuck with the discomfort of the rupture; connection itself becomes problematic. In order to re-establish connection in these circumstances, someone needs to show they understand how nobody's there to receive the call. In therapy, insisting on helpful presence when the felt experience is of preoccupied absence, paradoxically confirms the disconnection.

Responsive contingency then seems to be a crucial aspect of babies' formative experience, and also of effective therapy, when it can resonate with, reflect upon and respond to the actual qualities of someone's relational experience. The neurobiology suggests it is the patterning process, the flow of interaction, that seems to forge the connection, rather than any specific content at declarative level. Taking into account the anticipation machine of the mind of the child in therapy, the therapist tunes in and responds in the present moment. She resonates with the emotionality the child conveys – including that which is transferred into the present relationship from past relational experience. Just as implicit process, rather than explicit content, shapes the mind of the baby, the same process shapes the therapeutic encounter between resonating bodies and minds, and begins to make the therapeutic path from the old world into the new. This is the bewildering, beautiful, and burdensome process I tried to describe in *Being Taken In: The Framing Relationship* (Sutton, 2014).

Psychoanalysis has long attended to implicit emotional undercurrents, and some of its contemporary leading lights alert us to their value as a vital part not just of understanding but of therapeutic technique. In *Live Company*, Alvarez (1992) pioneers exploration of the presence of the other in co-creating a feeling of vitality and potential, swimming against the current sometimes of a psychoanalytic world in which absence was largely seen as the spur to thinking. Following Alvarez, Music (2014) argues for an adjustment of therapeutic technique when there are developmental deficits arising from abuse and neglect to do with regulation, processing, and thinking itself. His approach in these circumstances involves an emphasis on emotional regulation and implicit relational expectations. In *Nurturing Children* (2019), he writes of a paradigm shift in therapeutic work, involving an integration of neurobiological and developmental research with psychoanalysis, attachment theory, and systemic thinking. Lanyado (2004), working in the independent psychoanalytic tradition, focuses on the implicit qualities of the presence of the therapist, and with Horne (2006) has drawn on developmental research to illuminate clinical technique. Seligman (2017) too describes a new, developmentally informed psychoanalysis that tunes in to the lived experience of the body, paying special attention to non-verbal, emotional, and interactive communications.

Rayner (1992/2019) explains the lesson for therapeutic analysis from development research, that verbal communication alone is not enough when emotional structures with their pre-verbal roots are involved. He calls for attention to be paid to what is conveyed through rhythm, pace, and other elements of what may be described as the musical qualities of the encounter. This relates to Alvarez's (1993, 2012) ideas about making the thought thinkable. She writes of how, in order to reach 'memories in feeling – or worse, severe loss of feeling – we may have to go beyond words and consider the use of our emotional and even emotive countertransference responses' (2012:8). In *The Thinking Heart* (2012), she offers a structural schema for working with children at different levels of access to feeling, including an intensified vitalizing level for children who are chronically dissociated, despairing, or 'undrawn'. She describes the complex art of listening, and the need for careful attention to the quality of a child's brief glance which may 'offer a clue, a faint signal that can be amplified and built upon tactfully' (2012:164) at the right developmental level. On such foundations, she suggests, treatment may be built.

In going beyond words and listening to the music of what happens in the mother and baby relationship, Malloch attends to attributes of human communication that facilitate co-ordinated companionship, elements of 'communicative musicality' (1999). Mutual looks, vocalizations, and reciprocal movements begin to build connection, forming proto-conversations, patterns, and sequences that are taken in as dynamic forms of vitality and musicality, shaping the tempo and contours of a mutual flow of emotional expression. This flow goes before and beyond (though also through) language. Like a film score, it conveys mood and motive, pace, and timing. A sense of shared time can be created through the joint dynamic contours of these exchanges; phrases and cycles of feeling co-created in mutual musicality, involving anticipation of rhythm, and the impulse to move: 'the dance of wellbeing' (Trevarthen & Malloch, 2000). Given that a mental health symptom means this process did not go smoothly, the therapeutic dance must of course involve jarring and disharmonious elements in its flow.

Tronick describes a therapeutic model that draws on infancy research, rooted in the emotional communication of a shared relationship. It focuses on process rather than structure, and sees change as taking place in the implicit relationship at 'moments-of-meeting' through alterations in 'ways-of-being-with':

> It does not replace a past deficit. Rather something new is created in the relationship which alters the intersubjective environment. Past experience is recontextualized in the present such that a person operates from within a different mental landscape, resulting in new behaviours in the present and future.
>
> (2007:437–8)

Through the dynamic, contingent qualities of the new relationship, a response other than compliance with the terms of the old template for relating can be experienced, imagined, and begin to be lived out.

As Tronick explains, the qualities of attention in the new relational patterns can be taken in and new connections gradually thereby established. Alvarez (2012) gives a master class in therapeutic virtuosity, moving between explanatory, descriptive, and intensified vitalizing levels of work as aspects of the child in treatment come to light. They are revealed through her profound poetic attention to nuances in the emotional qualities of the transference and the whole therapeutic relationship, moment by moment in sessions. In line with the developmental research we have seen, she embodies and recommends a therapeutic response which is highly attuned, contingent upon the particular feeling of the child's expressive emotionality.

Giving disturbing feelings a new relational context seems to promote more lasting therapeutic change than ways of working that rely on trying to effect change solely at a cognitive level. In fact even if this were desirable, it would only ever be possible in a redacted account. Put two or more human beings in a room, and there will be communicative musicality. It just may not be written about. The feelings evidence, the musical qualities of the relational experience may be excluded from the received account. This is short-sighted, and actually turns out to be scientifically unsound. It seems from the wealth of research on the way the mind is formed that in order to establish new ways of understanding and relating to the world, we need to pay attention to the qualities of the process, rather than content – not just what is happening, but what it feels like.

Thinking outside the frame

Work on these implicit levels will find words to express discovered meanings, but it has become abundantly clear that our minds, even therapeutic minds, make retrospective sense of experience, instantly, through a number of experience-dependent filters. The primary relationship, which I have called a framing relationship (Sutton, 2014) because it builds a framework for experiencing the world, gives form through language to the feeling of what happens. Powerful impulses find expression through the body and are re-presented through resonance in the mother's body, and then represented in the expressions, words, and gestures she chooses to give shape to these impulses, depending on her own particular understanding of them. This understanding, the way in which attention is paid, and to what, has a shaping effect. Even in later life, we are influenced by the kind of attention paid; elderly people, for example, whose attention has been drawn to associations of wisdom and experience with old age perform better in memory tests than those primed with associations of senility and dementia (Levy, 1996).

In the verbal exchanges of the therapeutic encounter, the kind of attention paid and the language in which understandings are framed shape experience in a similar way. The minds of both people in the room explain what they think is happening after the event, in terms of a narrative they already recognize from their own framing relationships. Psychoanalysts' own careful analysis of these relationships, their templates for understanding the relational world, is crucial in helping them be open to new perspectives emerging out of new emotional information flowing through them; but it does not guarantee it. Midgley (2006) points out that the theoretical model used by the analyst structures what he or she sees in the data. We look to great figures of the past, our psychoanalytic parents, to let us know what could be happening. Yet Freud was clear that his work, though groundbreaking, would inevitably be provisional, open to revision as new research emerges which sheds light on the workings of the mind in ways he could not anticipate. Among others, Cozolino (2010) in *The Neuroscience of Psychotherapy* and Schore (2012) in *The Science of the Art of Psychotherapy* have taken up the baton.

It sometimes seems to be a challenge clinically to understand that the relational approach is a scientific one, and vice versa, using what is now known about the physiology of emotional communication to find ways of connecting and making new meanings. Neurobiology suggests that this meaning-making relationship in itself means a new meaning, a new sense of self, and a new template for relating become possible. Vorus (2018) explains how the meaning-making nature of the whole therapeutic relationship, rather than specifically verbal interpretation, lies at the core of therapeutic intervention. Meaning is not only to be discovered in the intention of the sender. I hope to have shown how, in a parallel with infancy, it is through the intention and understanding of the receiver too that new meanings can be made. Indeed, Alvarez (2012) differentiates a level of work involving an insistence on meaning itself, where a child is not so much in retreat as lost in a desert, needing to be recalled to the human family.

In the therapeutic relationship, then, taking the feeling of what happens as potential emotional communication about past (and therefore present) experience can be transformative. The therapeutic response needs to pay attention both to re-presented relational truths and to potential new ways of understanding them, gradually bringing both in an attuned way into the conversation, the relational story co-created between therapist and patient. In this way the past is no longer the only potential present and future.

Incorporating perspectives from other disciplines into new more relational and developmental clinical understandings is itself an example of such a move towards a different future for mental health clinicians, and brings many of the same fears we have seen earlier in relation to change – that of a disturbing loss of bearings. Ramachandran describes 'a widespread fear among scholars in the humanities and arts that science may one day take over their discipline …, a syndrome I have dubbed "neuron envy"' (2012:217). The fear Ramachandran describes may hold sway to some degree in psychoanalysis. Schore's (2012) work, though, particularly highlights complementarity and not polarity in the approaches of art and science. Research has shown how meaning-making acts as a psychobiological regulator, and how the stories of our lives are grounded in physiological responses that go back generations. Hobson (2002) too links the poetry of emotional experience with the prose of its study. He laments the banishment of drama and feeling in the search for explanations seen as 'scientific'. He eschews traditional psychological terms and describes with relish the way a baby is riveted by the blowing of bubbles, or how she delights in sharing the moment. These qualities are hard to measure in the bookkeeping double entry frame so often used as a default template for assessing value, and so they do not necessarily make the final edit, or even the first, in a left-hemisphere-friendly 'scientific' account of research into babyhood. Yet they are clearly part of our experience of babies, and theirs of themselves, and these are the qualities to which carers respond, through which minds are made. Hobson argues that 'if we are to understand that other people have subjective experiences (that is, a mind), we need to relate to people with feelings' (2002:251). In fact, of course, we have no choice.

In the search for truth, an art/science or any other either/or polarization inevitably excludes vital parts of the picture. We have seen how the disconnected left brain deletes or distorts information that does not fit the prevailing scheme. It discredits sensory and emotional information, conducting what McGilchrist calls an 'assault on our embodied nature' (2009:440). A fuller account of how minds develop needs to include insight from a range of points of view, and make connections with the right hemisphere, the seat of creativity and imagination, open to our embodied selves, and to new experience.

In the context of the widespread crisis of modern living expressed as a mental health epidemic, it is high time to widen our focus from the individual and build on the implications of the neurobiological research of recent decades, guided by researchers like Panksepp (1998), who alerts us to the play, seeking, fear, and other physiological systems we have in common with many mammals. We are social animals, and our feelings and behaviour are to be understood in our relational context. Our inherent adaptive relationality means that when someone's emotionality and behaviour does not seem to fit the current context, we need to try to understand and respond to messages implicitly conveyed from an earlier one. There will be a context; it just may not be about now. Rather, it may be transferred into now, in a way that can only be accessed through emotional resonance.

The development research then largely supports claims which may have been rejected by the scientific community in the past, but which are now coming into view as the cornerstone of any effective mental health treatment (Cozolino, 2010; Schore, 2012). Relational, transference, and countertransference-informed ways of working are validated by the research – provided the symptom is not personalized. Adam, for example, was suffering from his family's lack of capacity to mediate his father's death, from a maternal mind which was Teflon-coated as it were, protected against his mother's own troubling early experience, and experienced by him as convex, in Williams' (1997) term, rather than containing. The idea of the suicide had nowhere to go in the family, and so Adam carried it in his body. Maria suffered from her father's childhood, and his desperate need to protect a long gone beloved mother. Jacob's suicidality sprang from his family's incapacity to acknowledge and mourn the death of his mother; nobody could bear to know essential truths about his being. Aisha's distress and dysregulation arose in relation to her mother's preoccupation by unprocessed traumatic experience, in the absence of a responsive partner.

Each of the stories we have considered, representing thousands of children who are seen in mental health clinics annually (official statistics in England show 1 in 8 children between 5 and 19 years old had a mental health disorder in 2017), is a story about parents under pressure in a troubling family and/or wider social situation. We do children like them a disservice, and risk reinforcing despair, if we treat their symptoms as personal characteristics of their individual minds, rather than an implicit communication of the state in which they find themselves.

The neuroscience of the way human minds are adaptively wired has clear social and political implications, which are more properly the subject of another book; but it is worth mentioning here that it makes sense to invest in supporting relationships during a baby's first thousand days, which are by far the most formative. A degree of plasticity continues throughout life, though, and there is a second huge burst of connectivity during adolescence, when typically there needs to be a new adaptation to the environment as independence beckons. Therapy could never remove the need for social and emotional support for people suffering adversity, but once pressures have meant relational damage is done, then using models of therapy that start early and take modern neurobiology into account is simply more efficient, as well as humane.

It is clear then that understandings about the human self emerge from a conversation between perspectives. Far from being mutually exclusive, narrative and neurobiology make mutual connections. Even the most theatrical narratives are wired in through neurobiological connections that shape how we play out and understand the stories of our lives. Emotionality, the feeling of what happens, and musicality, its expression, are at the core of both. The science of relating highlights the formative nature of our connection with others, showing how the musicality of social communication in togetherness wires in patterns which form the groundwork for our very being. I hope to have shown just how crucial is the response of the other in establishing these sense- and story-making connections, in understanding, and naming the feeling of what happens. How it feels to be the way we are in our lives is conveyed body to body and mind to mind, whether we acknowledge it or not. As clinicians, we need to recognize the power implicit in naming the problem, and consider the impact on the child of being inaccurately regarded as the source of disturbance. When we realize that disturbance is not the property of an individual child, but a characteristic of relational experience, we can include the intergenerational constellation of mind-forming, meaning-making relationships around the child and family in our understanding of the relational story the symptom tells. Tuning in to the patterns of relating the symptom expresses, through our own embodied responses, means the dissonance between the score and the script in the story of distressed children's lives can, perhaps, finally be heard.

References

Akomfrah, J. (1986). *Handsworth Songs*. London: Black Audio Film Collective.

Alvarez, A. (1992). *Live Company: Psychoanalytic Psychotherapy with Autistic, Borderline, Deprived and Abused Children*. London: Routledge.

Alvarez, A. (1993). Making the thought thinkable: On introjection and projection. *Psychoanalytic Inquiry*, 13:103–122.

Alvarez, A. (2012). *The Thinking Heart: Three Levels of Psychoanalytic Therapy with Disturbed Children*. London: Routledge.

Balbernie, R. (2013). The importance of secure attachment for infant mental health. *Journal of Health Visiting*, 1(4):210–217.

Bornstein, M. H. (1989). *Maternal Responsiveness: Characteristics and Consequences*. San Francisco, CA: Jossey-Bass.

Cozolino, L. (2010). *The Neuroscience of Psychotherapy: Healing the Social Brain*. New York: Norton.

Damasio, A. (1999). *The Feeling of What Happens: Body and Mind in the Making of Consciousness*. Florida: Harcourt.

Felitti, V. J., Anda, R. F., Nordenberg, D., Williamson, D. F., Spitz, A. M., Edwards, V., Koss, M. P., & Marks, J. S. (1998). Relationship of childhood abuse and household dysfunction to many of the leading causes of death in adults. The Adverse Childhood Experiences (ACE) study. *American Journal of Preventative Medicine*, 14(4):245–258.

Fairbairn, W. R. D. (1946). Object-relationships and dynamic structure. *International Journal of Psychoanalysis*, 27:30–37.

Fraiberg, S., Adelson, E., & Shapiro, V. (1975). Ghosts in the nursery: A psychoanalytic approach to the problems of impaired infant-mother relationships. *Journal of the American Academy of Child & Adolescent Psychiatry*, 14(3):387–421.

Gallese, V. (2009). Mirror neurons, embodied simulation and the neural basis of social identification. *Psychoanalytic Dialogues*, 19:519–536.

Hobson, P. (2002). *The Cradle of Thought*. London: Macmillan.

Klein, M. (1952). The origins of transference. *International Journal of Psycho-Analysis*, 33:433–438.

Iacoboni, M. (2009). Imitation, Empathy, and Mirror Neurons. *Annual Review of Psychology*, 60:653–670.

Lanyado, M. (2004). *The Presence of the Therapist: Treating Childhood Trauma*. London: Routledge.

Lanyado, M. & Horne, A. (Eds.). (2006). *A Question of Technique: Independent Psychoanalytic Approaches with Children and Adolescents*. London: Routledge.

Levy, B. (1996). Improving memory in old age through implicit self-stereotyping. *Journal of Personality and Social Psychology*, 71(6):1092–1107.

Malloch, S. (1999). Mothers and infants and communicative musicality. *Musicae Scientiae: European Society for the Cognitive Sciences of Music*, 3 (1):29–57.

Mauritz, M. W., Goossens, P. J. J., Draijer, N., & van Achterberg, T. (2013). Prevalence of interpersonal trauma exposure and trauma-related disorders in severe mental illness. *European Journal of Psychotraumatology*, 4:10–25.

McGilchrist, I. (2009). *The Master and His Emissary: The Divided Brain and the Making of the Western World*. New Haven, CT:Yale.

Melzak, S. & McClatchey, J. (2019). Exploring community, cultural, developmental and trauma rooted barriers to mourning after times of organised violence and war. *Journal of Child Psychotherapy*, 44(3):396–415.

Midgley, N. (2006). Re-reading 'Little Hans': Freud's case study and the question of competing paradigms in psychoanalysis. *Journal of the American Psychoanalytic Association*, 54(2):537–559.

Murray, L. & Trevarthen, C. (1986). The infant's role in mother-infant communications. *Journal of Child Language*, 13(1):15–29.

Music, G. (2014). Top down and bottom up: Trauma, executive functioning, emotional regulation, the brain and child psychotherapy. *Journal of Child Psychotherapy*, 40(1):3–19.

Music, G. (2019). *Nurturing Children: From Trauma to Growth using Attachment Theory, Psychoanalysis and Neurobiology*. London: Routledge.

Panksepp, J. (1998). *Affective Neuroscience: The Foundations of Human and Animal Emotions*. New York: Oxford University.

Perry, B. D. (2001a). The neurodevelopmental impact of violence in childhood. In D. Schetky & E. P. Benedek (Eds.), *Textbook of Child and Adolescent Forensic Psychiatry*:221–238. Washington, DC: American Psychiatric.

Perry, B. D., Hambrick, E. P., Brawner, T. W., Brandt, K., Hofmeister, C., & Collins, J. (2018). *Beyond the ACE score: Examining relationships between timing of developmental adversity, relational health and developmental outcomes in children Archives of Psychiatric Nursing*. Retrieved from www.researchgate.net/publication/328833363_Beyond_the_ACE_score_Examining_relationships_between_timing_of_developmental_adversity_relational_health_and_developmental_outcomes_in_children.

Perry, B. D., Pollard, R. A., Blakley, T. L., Baker, W. L., & Vigilante, D. (1995). Childhood trauma, the neurobiology of adaptation, and 'use dependent' development of the brain: How 'states' become 'traits'. *Infant Mental Health Journal*, 16(4):271–291.

Ramachandran, V. S. (2012). *The Tell-Tale Brain: Unlocking the Mystery of Human Nature*. London: Random.

Rayner, E. (1992/2019). Matching, attunement and the psychoanalytic dialogue. In J. Edwards (Ed.)*Psychoanalysis and Other Matters: Where are We Now?* London: Routledge.

Rosenfeld, H. (1964). On the psychopathology of narcissism: A clinical approach. *International Journal of Psychoanalysis*, 45:332–337.

Schore, A. N. (1996). The experience-dependent maturation of a regulatory system in the orbital prefrontal cortex and the origin of developmental psychopathology. *Development and Psychopathology*, 8(1):59–87.

Schore, A. N. (2010). The right brain implicit self: A central mechanism of the psychotherapy change process. In J. Petrucelli (Ed.), *Knowing, Not-knowing and Sort of Knowing: Psychoanalysis and the Experience of Uncertainty*:177–202. London: Karnac.

Schore, A. N. (2012). *The Science of the Art of Psychotherapy*. New York: Norton.

Seligman, S. (2017). *Relationships in Development: Infancy, Intersubjectivity, and Attachment*. New York: Routledge.

Sutton, S. (2014). *Being Taken In: The Framing Relationship*. London: Karnac.

Trevarthen, C. & Malloch, S. (2000). The dance of wellbeing: Defining the musical therapeutic effect. *The Nordic Journal of Music Therapy*, 9(2):3–17.

Tronick, E. (2007). Noninterpretive mechanisms in psychoanalytic therapy: The 'something more' than interpretation. In E. Tronick (Ed).*The Neurobehavioral and Social-Emotional Development of Infants and Children*:418–438. Norton: New York.

van der Kolk, B. (1989). The compulsion to repeat the trauma re-enactment, revictimization, and masochism. *Psychiatric Clinics of North America*, 12 (2):389–411.

Vorus, N. (2018). Theory of mind and therapeutic action: A contemporary freudian integration. In C. Bonovitz & A. Harlem (Eds.), *Developmental Perspectives in Child Psychoanalysis and Psychotherapy*. New York: Routledge, 158–180.

Williams, G. (1997). *Internal Landscapes and Foreign Bodies: Eating disorders and other pathologies*. London: Routledge.

Index